The Streets Don

The Streets Don't Love You Back

The Streets Don't Love You Back

The Streets Don't Love You Back

Author

Robert D. Boyd Jr.

The Streets Don't Love You Back

The Streets Don't Love You Back

Edited

By

Lucinda F. Boyd

The Streets Don't Love You Back

The Streets Don't Love You Back

Copyright © 2008 Robert D. Boyd Jr.
First Printing: 2008
ISBN 978-1-5136-0380-3

The Streets Don't Love You Back

The Streets Don't Love You Back

Robert D. Boyd Jr.

The Streets Don't Love You Back

**This book is dedicated to my stepfather
Aaron Hardin Jr., Passed March 5, 1973**

I have always missed you more than words can say. You are the only father that I knew and loved. You took care of me and taught me many things. When you died a part of me died as well and that's when my life fell apart. My birth father has still never been a part of my life. I thank God for my Mothers strength and prayers, I have been able to change my life and become successful. Thank you for all you did for me. Rest in Peace Daddy.

The Streets Don't Love You Back

To my Manager, Lucinda F. Boyd

Thank you very much for getting behind my career, believing in me, and in "The Streets Don't Love You Back Movement." Thank you for the many long hours of typing, editing and revising that you put into my book. I will always love you for believing in me. May God bless your life!

Sincerely, Rob Boyd
2009

The Streets Don't Love You Back

My name is Robert D. Boyd Jr. I was born at Detroit Memorial Hospital. My parents are Vernon Guyton Boyd and Robert D. Boyd Sr. I grew up on the east side of Detroit in Michigan.

We lived on a street called Galster from the time I was born until I was nine years old. We lived next to the Womack family. My mother and Mrs. Womack were best friends. If I wasn't home I could be found at the Womack home or playing baseball out in the street or back yard with neighborhood friends.

I came from a big family my mom has thirteen sisters and one brother. We were not rich but the love we had for each other out weighed all other things. I was raised primarily by my mom.

My stepfather took care of my sister and I just as if we were his own, he used to take me to the Y.M.C.A. where I learned to box and swim. My stepfather was the only daddy we knew as young children.

My real father wasn't in my life much, the times he was in my life he would stand me up and when I was older my father rejected me and told my mom —he's in that gang life and I don't want any part of that.

My mother would tell me how successful he was and I would hear him on the radio and see him on television. I always wondered if he had so much money, then why didn't he ever do anything for us and my Mama had to work three jobs to take care of us.

I remember when my dad had called my mom and told her to bring me down to the church where he was preaching that day. Dad was going to give me money for a pair of shoes. We had to walk all the way down there near the railroad tracks, we get to the church and he is up there preaching. After the service, we go out front to wait and meet him but he never showed up, he went out the side door of the church and left without even speaking to us or giving us the money for shoes.

I was hurt so bad that day, he stood us up and all I needed was a pair of shoes and mom couldn't afford them. The worst part of it was that mom had faith in him and his word was bond. She walked me all the way to that church to see him and he left us hanging.

I remember the time that he said he was going take me to a baseball game; I loved baseball and wanted to be a baseball player someday. I could have been a baseball player; I was good at it and could play any position. Dad took that desire away from me when he stood me up at the stadium that day. I waited so long that eventually a man came out and asked me, —lil fella, who are you waiting for? "I said I'm waiting for my

13

dad, he told me to meet him here but he has not shown up yet".

The man then said, "come on in son and finish watching the game". As I sat there that day, watching the Detroit -vs- N.Y. game, I felt that I never wanted to play or even go to another game. I had gotten used to Dad letting me down and was so discouraged I told myself —forget him. I will be the man of the house and take care of us. I went home and told Mom, she replied, I'm going to take care of you the best way I can, if he doesn't want to give you any money then that's on him. One thing I can truly say is that my Mother has never talked bad about my real dad. Mom would say that God will work it out when the time is right. That time is now.

Throughout this book, you will see the difficulties, the heartache and hardships that I endured as a young child. You will also see how my life could have been very different. I needed my father all my life and he was not there for me. Fathers and Mothers do not let your children grow up without your good and constant guidance. They need us more than ever now. After you read this book go hug your children and let them know that you love them and no matter what you will always be in their lives to help and guide them.

TRAGEDY HITS MY LIFE AT NINE YEARS OLD

The year was March 1973, when tragedy struck and changed my life forever. It was a very cold night and my stepfather had just got off work. I was happy he was home because he always used to bring us something good to eat home with him.

This night my stepfather and mother were having words about something. I heard them arguing so I came out of my room. My stepfather was not abusive and would never put his hands on my mother.

Little did I know that my mom's sister who lived in the same house with us had called upstairs to my grandfather and had told grandfather that mom and dad were fighting, my grandfather came downstairs and was very angry; he was always overprotective of his girls. He kept telling my stepfather to leave and my stepfather would not leave. I was still standing outside their door looking in; my mother was sitting on the side of her bed along with my stepfather. My stepfather was tired and just wanted to go to bed. This is where it all went bad.

Before I knew it, my grandfather had stabbed my stepfather to death, I will never forget the blood, the anger and my mom crying and screaming. I will never forget my mom screaming at me —get some towels, he's bleeding to death!

This was the first time I had ever seen anyone get killed. My stepfather died in my mother's arms. From that point on, I became cold towards people and life in general.

I hated my grandfather for what he had done. I remember the next day reading in the newspaper and seeing my grandfather's picture. I hated him so much for taking my stepfathers life. My mom was very sad it almost destroyed her life. My grandfather would not let the police ask me any questions about what happened that night. My grandfather did not serve any time in jail for killing my stepfather. I was in shock and I knew I was going to have to make things happen for me and my family. From this day on my life became very private. I remember the day of the funeral; my mother had helped me get dressed. At the funeral I cried more than ever in my life. It was one of the saddest days and I remember thinking what am I going to do now. Mom packed us up and we moved to a street called Strong. This is where my life as "Lil Rob" began. I became the man of the house; mom was pregnant with my baby brother Dwight who my stepfather would never see. Dwight was born August 1973. We then moved into a gang infested neighborhood.

We lived just west of the church on Strong Street.
The house we lived in is not there now.

The Streets Don't Love You Back

At the age of ten, I remember that I was on my way to school and was robbed by a gang member not much older than I, he took my coat and it was cold outside.

I was mad as hell that I had lost my stepfather, I didn't have a relationship with my biological father and now some big guy takes my coat from me. I ran back to my neighborhood and told some of the older guys what had just happened. Come to find out they knew the guy that had robbed me because he was from another gang. At the age of ten, I did not realize this was a gang neighborhood. Immediately they wanted me to join their gang, The Bishop Gang and the other big gang was the "Chain Gang." The Bishop gang went to get my coat back, in order for me to be a part of the crew I had to pistol whip the guy who robbed me of my coat. From that day on guys began to fear me on the Eastside of Detroit. We were always gang banging and staying in trouble. The crew territory was Van Dyke and Harper but I hung out in the Warren and Conner Projects and the Brewster Projects.

Brewster Projects

The Streets Don't Love You Back

Since I did not have either father in my life the gang became my family and father figures. I started looking to the older "cats", they would ask me, "are you willing to lose your life over this" All I could say is that "it doesn't matter" I just had to take care of my mother, three younger brothers and my sister no matter what. I was willing to give my life to do so.

At 10 years old I should have been in school, but I would meet up with my crew as soon as we met at school. I ended up being kicked out of many schools in Detroit. We would hustle on the street corner all day and mess with girls. I remember when I was twelve years old I had my first girlfriend and she became the mother of my son. I was just fourteen years old when my son was born. Michael Boyd was born in August 1978, I was very happy but at that time my life was already out of control. I didn't know anything about taking care of a baby as I was still a child myself.

The Streets Don't Love You Back

We used to hang out at the nineteenth hole and gamble.

When I was 14, we were in school at Burroughs Jr. High and got into a fight with a rival gang. I pulled out my gun and started shooting up the school. The cops came and shut down the whole neighborhood. No one would tell them that Lil Rob did the shooting. I eventually turned myself in and was arrested. My Mother bailed me out and after only seven hours was in trouble again. I had run into a homeboy that had recently crossed me and I pulled my gun out and started shooting. The cops picked me up once again and I spent eight months in jail. I later got in trouble for stealing cars. I had always been in trouble; my mother constantly worried about me and would have to come see about me. I started being locked up at the age of twelve and ended up in a boy's home for troubled youth. I stayed in so much trouble that the state of Michigan took me from my mother and made me a ward of the state. I stayed in several group homes for troubled teenagers. No matter how much trouble I got in, my mother was always there and never turned her back on me. Mama would always say, Bobby I have to put you in God's hands,

The Streets Don't Love You Back

because he's the only one that can touch you, and I can't wait for God to change your life. My mother ended up raising Michael and me, although Michael lived with me he still always had contact with his mother.

I lived the gang life for many years and were friends with some of the most dangerous drug dealers and gangsters in Detroit. I have seen a lot of hurt, death and destruction over the years. It was all about power, money, cars and women.

In 1980 when I got out of jail I went down to Warren and Conner Projects where my cousin Darryl was hustling. Darryl was glad to see me and asked, "What's up" I said, "what's going on" Darryl said —do you want to make some money? I said —hell yeah what's up? Darryl said —I know you just got out but are you still putting in work? I said —you know that cuz. Then he asked me if I would be his Enforcer and I said

The Streets Don't Love You Back

—damn it's like that cuz... he said —yeah we can make lots of money.

We started the 430 Crew and from that point on I worked with my cousin until 1984 when we had a falling out.

In 1982 I was at a club with Darryl and our bodyguard named Space. Darryl got in an altercation with another man because of the girl he was talking to. I came to see what was going on and when I turned my back was stabbed in the back with a hook knife. My bodyguard shot the whole place up and then took me to the hospital. I had already lost so much blood and was unconscious and at one time stopped breathing and had to be resuscitated. I survived but was weak and had to use crutches for four months to help me walk.

There were times that we would take the whole crew to the mall and spend $10,000-$20,000 on clothes and food.

Let me remind you that Darryl was my first cousin and he crossed me on some money ($500,000). Darryl knew how I got down therefore; by him being family I gave him a pass. I started finding out that he was messing up the money and was even using his own product. That hurt me to find out that he was doing that. Darryl's brother Larry —Fab was also a member of the 430 crew.

We gave him his start in the heroin business and he later branched out on his own and became his own boss and made millions. In 2000 my cuz, Fab died of an accidental drug overdose. Rest in Peace.

The Streets Don't Love You Back

Darryl "Dijon" Jackson 1986

Co-Founder of the 430 Crew

The Streets Don't Love You Back

Larry "Fab" Thompson
430 Crew and later Boss of his own crew

The Streets Don't Love You Back

Ski-bo and Fab in younger years 1982

The Streets Don't Love You Back

Darryl Jackson, Darryl Brown Sylvester "Sonny" Long,
Sonny's cousin and Robert Boyd 1982

The Streets Don't Love You Back

Steve Washington, (later killed in Detroit's Eastside)
Cliff Jones on right, Rob Boyd's Best Man 1985

Now as the Boss I continued running the 430 Crew. Darryl later died in 2001 also of a drug overdose. I hooked up with Cliff Jones who had recently been released from prison on a six year sentence in a murder case. Cliff and I did some hustling together. Cliff was one of my best men at my wedding in 1985 and paid $10,000 for my wedding.

We remained friends although going our own ways and I left town in 1989. Cliff is currently doing Life in prison. The other best man at my wedding was Rock, who paid for the

The Streets Don't Love You Back

Rolls Royce. Rock found a good job and is still currently employed with the same company 24 years later.

Cliff Jones, Rob Boyd, 1985 at Robs Wedding

Rock, with Rob Boyd 2009

The Streets Don't Love You Back

Rob Boyd, Gloria, Greg, Cliff Jones 1985

The Streets Don't Love You Back

To all the brothers of the Bishop Crew, As you know I did not have a relationship with my birth father and moved into the neighborhood after witnessing the murder of my step-father. You were there for me when I did not have a father. All of you became my brothers, my family. Right or wrong you had my back, you taught me, and guided me for many years. Much love and respect to: Butch, Darryl and Rob Brown; Timmy, Steve, Keke, Charles, Gino and Bird Rucker; Uncle Ash and Sirone Sims; Cheese and Donnie Corbin; Charley; Blade and Wayne Weatherington; Frank: Michael Kirk, Vick, Fred, Peanut, Bruce and Wayne, Tuck, Rooster, Marco, Snoop, Joe, Dobb, Cowboy, Punchie, Woo, Little William and Bulldog, Big A, Tommy Hunter, Little Terrance. To all of my homeboys wherever you may be and for those who always kept it 100 may God bless you. Ya'll know who you are.

Mike, Chris, Rob Boyd, Bulldog and Disco at the club.

The Streets Don't Love You Back

Maserati" Rick Carter

*Rob Boyd's friend Orville, Ex-Kingpin from
Eastside of Detroit, doing life in Prison.
Orville also hung around with White Boy Rick.*

The Streets Don't Love You Back

CLIFFORD JONES
THE CLIFF JONES DRUG ORGANIZATION

From 1984 until 1993, Clifford Jones operated the most feared band of thugs and outlaws in the city of Detroit. Jones got his start in the drug operation of Demetrius Holloway but quickly branched out forming his own murder for hire gang.

Jones was a fearsome presence on the streets of Detroit that authorities had a hard time getting anyone to even acknowledge that they had even heard of him.

The Jones gang was known for carrying out ruthless and efficient executions on behalf of many of Detroit's drug kingpins. The Jones group practiced the art of murder yet lacked the discipline of some of the other organizations run by Demetrius Holloway and Maserati Rick Carter.

One of Jones favorite tactics was to carry out a contract for a drug dealer, receive his payment and then murder the client and steal his supply narcotics. Near the end of his gangs reign

The Streets Don't Love You Back

Jones made an attempt to take over a law firm in hopes of gaining an in house counsel while getting information on how to launder his gang's proceeds. This went all wrong as federal and state investigators closed in on Jones and his thugs in February of 1993. After a sensational trial which lay at least fifty drugs related killings on the Jones boys. Clifford was sentenced to life in the Federal Prison system I also reconnected with friend, Maserati Rick Carter. I had grown up with Rick, his brother Greg and brother Clyde.

We all use to box at the same gym (Crock's Gym) Rick and I had always wanted to be champion boxers, we used to train with Thomas Hearn's at the gym and Don King would be there on many occasions talking to Emmanuel Steward, Thomas Hearn's manager.

I boxed for four years on Junction in the West side of Detroit. Mom would always encourage me and say that anything is possible.

The Streets Don't Love You Back

Greg Carter, (Maserati Rick's brother) Rob Boyd and another friend at Pat's Lounge September 10, 1987

The Streets Don't Love You Back

RICHARD CARTER
FOUNDER BEST FRIENDS
1977-1988

Maserati Rick

During the height of Detroit's crack craze, Maserati Rick Carter reigned as the most recognized of all of the flashy, high rolling dealers in the motor city. None could match Rick's flair for the dramatic an attribute he would display even in death. Rick Carter first came to the attention of local authorities when at the age of 18 he drew a conviction for receiving stolen property. It would be five years before Carter became a player in the cities drug trade. Originally a small timer with big dreams Carter's ascent began with the fall of Sylvester "Seal" Murray in 1982. Murray had been the prime source of cocaine; heroin and marijuana for scores of inner city the chief supplier for Detroit's first big time crack gang Y.B.I. The conviction of Murray along with the top leaders of

The Streets Don't Love You Back

Y.B.I. provided an opportunity for ambitious young men such as Carter and his best friend Demetrius Holloway to move into position as the new generation of drug pushers. After three short years in the crack trade, Maserati Rick controlled one of the most prominent networks operating on the east side. Carter and Holloway worked the eastside peacefully along with other organizations run by Johnny Curry whose wife Cathy was the niece of Detroit's Mayor Coleman Young, the remnants of the crippled Y.B.I., gang and the Chambers brothers. Following the arrest and conviction of the Curry brothers and 6 of their top lieutenants in 1987,

Rick and his partner Holloway began making overtures to secure the east side as their personal kingdom. One of the first steps in consolidating their power was to join forces with teenage drug supplier "White Boy" Rick Wershe while financing the organization of "Rockin" Reggie Browns murder for hire troop under the umbrella of best friends. With Brown providing much needed protection and muscle and Wershe providing a local source of product, Carter began expanding his operation by providing an alternative to his crack with heroin. Federal agents took note of Carter's frequent trips to Florida and Los Angeles in an attempt they claim to secure a steady supply source. Carter's operation took off allowing him to live and spend lavishly. Carter listed his home address as a bungalow on Birwood Avenue in northwest Detroit but he was known to have kept residence in at least two other locations in the last four years of his life. These two locations were more in line with the image Carter was building for himself as the motor city king of crack. The first was a fortified flat near Alter road and East Jefferson while the other a plush riverfront condo provided Carter with an occasional getaway. To mask the proceeds of his drug operation, Carter invested millions in local businesses many of which were eastside carwashes or hair salons which served as drop off or pickup points for his runners.

The Streets Don't Love You Back

Investigator's listed Carter as a kilo man in its reports on Detroit's many traffickers meaning he dealt in 2.2 lb. quantities of cocaine and heroin. This method of dealing signified his wealth and importance demonstrated by the fact that only the important traffickers and wealthy could afford to inventory such quantities without extreme financial difficulty. During his climb to prominence, Carter and his gang as one law enforcement official put it, made enough enemies to fill Tiger Stadium, but none seemed more determined to destroy Carter than Edward Hanserd, a man who had once bought his marijuana from Maserati Rick. Following a heated argument over a debt owed to Carter in Hanserd's Unisex Hair Salon during the summer of 1987, the two became bitter enemies. Carter and Hanserd publicly squared off on numerous occasions usually resulting in an exchange of automatic gunfire between the combatants. The initial war of words drew the attention of newsmen who wrote often of the exploits of both men whose violence coupled with a preference for automatic weaponry posed a grave danger to the general public. As Hanserd built and organization which began to cut into the profits of Carter and best friends the upstart was marked for termination a fact best demonstrated by an impromptu meeting which resulted in a wild shootout between the two dealers and a couple of their soldiers which left Hanserd with a nasty scar across his abdomen the result of a wound he received from a confrontation with Carter and his forces. Maserati Rick would try at least three times to kill the troublesome Hanserd without success. The failure of Carter to eliminate Hanserd would be a fatal mistake after yet another conflict on September 12, 1989 outside of one of Carter's businesses left Rick hospitalized with bullets in his stomach and one of Hanserd's soldiers slightly wounded in the arm. Two days after the initial shooting the same man involved in the initial shooting entered room 307 at Mt. Carmel Mercy Hospital and fired at least one shot into the head and face of Maserati Rick. Carter was pronounced dead at 6:01p.m. The next day police announced their prime suspect was Ricky Parker an associate of Hanserds who was fast establishing himself as the single most dangerous man on the eastside of Detroit. Just hours after the death of Carter, it was learned that another man whom he had been having a bitter feud with intended to call Rick as a defense witness in a trial he claimed was the result of a Carter initiated frame up.

Testimony puts suspect at murder site

By David Kocieniewski
News Staff Writer

Defendant Lodrick Parker ran from "Maserati Rick" Carter's hospital room carrying a handgun, moments before Carter was found shot to death Sept. 12 in a bed in Mt. Carmel Mercy Hospital, according to testimony Tuesday in 36th District Court.

Police contend Parker was hired to kill Carter, a reputed major east side Detroit cocaine dealer, in a drug turf war.

Parker's attorney, Rene Cooper, described his client as "a family man" who was not involved in Carter's death.

THE TESTIMONY came at a preliminary hearing before 36th District Judge Patrick Donahue, who ordered Parker to stand trial on charges of first-degree murder and use of a firearm during a felony.

No trial date has been set.

A former Mt. Carmel Mercy patient, who testified Tuesday, said she was in a hallway near Carter's room at 5:25 p.m. when she saw the suspect walk into the room.

A few seconds later, the woman testified, she heard a shot and saw Parker run from the room carrying a chrome-plated revolver.

"He came running down the hall and almost knocked me over," the woman said.

"Then he stopped and said, 'Someone's in there shooting.' Then he put the gun under his belt, and covered it up with his sweater and ran away."

Cooper cross-examined the witness for nearly two hours and cited four contradictions between her court testimony and a written statement she signed after the shooting.

AN AUTOPSY found that Carter, 29, died from a single gunshot wound to the face. At the time of his death, he was in the hospital recovering from a gunshot wound to the abdomen.

Police theorize a hit man first wounded Carter two days before in an unsuccessful murder attempt, then finished the job in the hospital.

Carter's funeral drew publicity when he was buried in a $16,000 custom casket made to resemble his Mercedes-Benz.

He was known as "Maserati Rick" — not because he drove the pricey Italian sports cars, but because of his flashy style and expensive tastes.

Assistant Prosecutor Michael Cruskin asked reporters not to identify witnesses in the case because he fears for their safety.

The Streets Don't Love You Back

Following his murder the legend of Maserati Rick Carter received its finishing touches during a grand funeral in which he lay in a $16,000 silver coffin constructed to resemble a Mercedes Benz complete with spinning tires. Following the emotional services Maserati Rick Carter was laid to rest in Mt. Carmel cemetery the final resting place of thousands of underworld figures including the royalty of Detroit's powerful partnership.

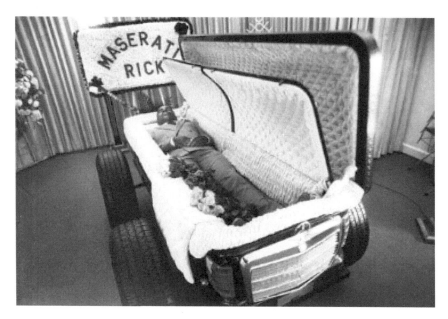

The Streets Don't Love You Back

Maserati Rick with Friends at Detroit Club

The Streets Don't Love You Back

I continued the 430 Crew with my homeboy, Sylvester Long and kept hustling together until he got caught in a murder case in 1985. I also married and things were looking up for me. I was trying to get away from the street and gang life. I thought that getting married would be the best thing for me, but it was not. We had a son, Robert in January 1989 and don't get me wrong, she was a good woman we just didn't see eye to eye on things and later got a divorce.

Sylvester was sentenced to a 15 year prison sentence and I continued the thug life for four more years, I couldn't seem to shake the street life until I started seeing all my homeboys getting killed or locked up in prison. When Rick (Maserati Rick) and Meat (Demetrius) got killed things started getting really crazy in the streets. Everybody in the streets was beefing over their deaths. My Best Man Cliff Jones (C.J.) got locked up for 20 years.

LEAVING DETROIT

I decided to leave Detroit in search of a better life. I remember going to my mother's house and telling her that I was leaving Detroit, and that if I didn't leave I would end up dead or doing life in prison. Mother was crying and asked where I was going. I told her a place called Cincinnati; I had taken the boys there every year for the Jazz Festival. I hate to see mom cry but I think they were tears of joy that I was leaving the hood. I was so tired of hurting my mom from the life I was living she was always a good woman. She had never been a drinker or smoker, never did any drugs. There are not too many people who can say that about their mother. Mom asked me how long I would be gone. I said maybe a year or longer I do not know yet. The next day I got a one way ticket and rode the Greyhound Bus to the −Nati, the only friend I had in Cincinnati picked me up at the bus station. He took me to their house in Forest Park, Ohio and I stayed with them for about four months. He and his wife were very positive people

The Streets Don't Love You Back

in my life and were good to me. They talked to me about church and changing my life. They planted the seed in me that would change my life forever. It was strange living in a different city where I did not have my family or my homeboys. All I had was GOD to depend on.

CHANGE

I never knew what it was like to work, my friend and his wife kept telling me that in order to change then I had to do what's right and that is to get a job and work for what you want. —God is going to bless you, because you have a genuine heart and are a good person.

I moved into my own apartment and I went from making that —one way money to waiting for a weekly paycheck. It was very hard but I kept hearing God's voice in my head telling me that I would have to go through this. It was like God telling me that he rode with me when I was doing things that I shouldn't have done and he always protected me from harm. Now God was going to ride with me and change my life and you will see his hand moving through the rest of my journey.

REAL JOBS

In 1990 my first job was in Cincinnati as a dishwasher at McDonald's on McMillan and Victory Park, I got a second job at Hardees and worked both jobs until 1991. I remember thinking how does a gangster turn into a dishwasher let alone a cook for just chump change.

I prayed to God —whatever you have for me must be good because this is hard for me Father.

I moved into a one bedroom apartment in Mt. Washington. I was getting used to working two jobs so I got two new jobs in Beechmont close to where I lived. The first job was at Arby's

The Streets Don't Love You Back

where I became a certified meat cutter and the second job was at Skyline Chile at Cherry Grove.

This was a neighborhood that did not have any black people except me. I started to adapt to the changes that were going on in my life. I was having so much fun with the people I was working with. I had never had fun around people that was not my family. They did not know anything about the man they were laughing and playing with, a man that had seen so much money and so much pain in his life it was so unreal and they knew nothing of me or my past. I use to like to get up and get ready for work, because the people I became friends with made me feel so comfortable and welcome and accepted me for me.

We used to play pool, go swimming at their houses.

I was stepping out into a normal life. I was becoming happier with my new life. I met a woman who was ten years older than me; I always thought older women had their lives together and know what they wanted. We would go out different places and have fun. She would always tell me, "you are a very private person", why don't you ever talk about yourself or your life? I would always tell her that there is nothing to talk about except the here and now. She had three children, one son and two daughters and we had a good relationship. Just as well, as I had a dark past, she had a lot going on in her life that I knew nothing about. She was going through a lot with her ex, she had left him but he couldn't accept that and was harassing her in front of the children. I finally told −get ya'll stuff and move in with me at my apartment. I know I did not have enough room but we made it work.

Times got hard and I had gotten sick for a couple of weeks. I had lost one job and the other reduced my hours. This was a mess now, how was I going to take care of these children and us?

The Streets Don't Love You Back

Well, a guy at the job told me that he knew of a way for me to make some fast money. We really needed it at the time, just like when I had to help my mom after my stepfather was murdered. I had to step up and be a man so once again, I was faced with what you would do to take care of your family.

Well you already know what I'm about to say. Yes, I put it down and did what I do, my family had to eat and bills had to be paid. I asked my girl to marry me, she said —yes and we were married in December 1992.

I thought that what I had done wasn't out of greed or selfishness but to feed my wife and kids. I felt bad and knew that I was doing what I had asked God to take me away from in Detroit. I realized I had made the wrong choice and was going to quit. I kept getting calls from my hook up but I didn't answer the phone I didn't want to live that kind of life anymore. We really needed some money and I told myself I'd do it just one more time so I answered the call. My hook up told me to meet him at the grocery store lot. We linked up and did the switch. I made twenty four hundred dollars; he had what he needed and was off. I had no idea that he had been busted a couple of months before. He went on his way and I went mine. Just then —Damn! The boys pull up right behind me and tell me to get out of the car. I was surrounded with nowhere to go.

Have you ever been in a position where your whole life passes before your eyes? My girl, my kids, oh my lord, my mother, Damn! I have to call mom and break her heart once again. I have to call my girl and let her know I'm in a hell of a mess. I was arrested in Mt. Washington and they sent me to Clermont County. I'm not sure how I ended up in their custody but was in that cell for four days until they let me out on bond. I found a lawyer who was not handling his business so I dropped him and a friend of mine, Tony Palazzolo said he would try to help me get a good lawyer so that I would have a fair trial. Man, I met this guy named Tony back in 1991; he had a jewelry store called Ounce O'Gold. I used to go to the store just to talk to him. He was one of the most positive men I had met in my life. I can say that to this day I love him. He and his wife took me in and treated me as a son. This Italian, Sicilian couple are the most beautiful people I have ever met. He is now my pops and she is my mom, their whole family shows me the love. I am so blessed to have them in my life and thank God for them.

In March 1993 a new lawyer called me; he had all my paper work and knew all about my case. In April I found a job in downtown Cincinnati at the Western Hotel. I would get off work at the Western Hotel and feel good that I found another job. Things seemed to be looking good for us again, we moved into a bigger place. One day I received a letter from my lawyer saying that he needed to talk to me. Tony and I went to the Lawyers office and he told us that I could get 15-20 years and that I should just plead guilty, and to accept what they're going to give me. He went on to say that if I take it to trial then that's costing more money and wasting time and the verdict was going to be the same.

SENTENCING

The day comes for me to go to court and the judge says, I can sentence you right now Mr. Boyd, I said, "yes sir". The judge said, I'm going to give you a 30 day P.S.I. (you get to go home and get things in order before your sentencing). The worst part about it was coming home and not knowing how long I was going to stay locked up when I go back. I did many things with my family while I had the chance. I prayed to God, I knew it was my fault and that I brought this upon myself.

On July 28, 1993 Tony comes to my house and picked me up for court, I kissed my wife goodbye and told her that I would be back soon.

The Streets Don't Love You Back

Now I am back in front of the judge and he has my whole life in his hands. God was the only one that knew what the judge was going to say. The judge finally said, Mr. Boyd, due to your charges, I sentence you to ten years in Prison. My heart sank —WOW, why is this happening to me. I had changed my life and only did what I did to care for my family. I knew that God was there for me and I felt that he had a purpose for me and a job he wanted to me to do.

I was then handcuffed and escorted to jail. I looked at Tony and I said, —I will see you when I get out. I was taken to Clermont County Jail where I stayed for fourteen days waiting for them to ship me out. The fourteenth day they took me to the C.R.C., a holding facility where you wait until they figure out which prison you are going to. As we pulled up to this facility I said to myself, —what did I get myself into, this is a misunderstanding. The guard was yelling at us saying —get the fuck off the bus I thought, these fool are crazy up in here. As we get through the gates we were told to strip off our clothes. I felt violated that another man could make me do this. We were then given a towel to wrap around us until we received our prison clothes.

They sent us to a spot called R-1; there you can only take a shower once a week on Saturdays. I was in this facility for two weeks and couldn't wait to leave there. The day came to move to another facility, now it's on to the R-2 facility where I can shower but have no soap to do so. I stayed there for two more weeks.

PRISON LIFE

One day the guard came to my cell and said, "Pack your stuff, you are moving". I said, "Moving where?" He said, "You're moving to the prison where you will do the rest of your time". The facility was P.C.I. in Columbus Ohio. While there

The Streets Don't Love You Back

I met a guy by the name of Drake, he did not talk too much. One day I got a chance to start a conversation with him, he was from Detroit. He asked me how I got caught up and ended up here. I told him I was set up by a guy on a drug deal.

He talked about his case, he was from Cleveland and his first case was back in 1983 when he shot someone and did three years flat on a three to fifteen year sentence that was running wild. Drake had gotten out in 1991 and he went back to his old ways hanging in the dope spots. Drake made it to the end of his parole and when it was time to sign release papers a red flag came across his parole officer's computer with a statement saying that Drake had been seen at a dope spot. They hand cuffed him and sent him back to prison to serve two more years.

I'm thinking now just because he was seen at a dope spot, he has to do two more years. That's what happens when change isn't in the big picture.

He told me many crazy stories about how young boys are treated when they come in here thinking that they are all that and they can't be touched. Then the bad boy comes and punks him straight out, now little man got to pay the brothers to keep the "dogs" off him. Then there are those who are liars and come to jail and lie about their case because they don't want you to know the real reason they are there. I met a guy that said he was there for drug charges but he was there because he raped a child. Coming to prison, this is the time to find out who you really want in your corner.

Then there are the people who started out with you but have their own life on the outside. You are looking for them to keep answering the collect phone calls, but they can't afford it, when you are on the inside you feel that everyone on the outside is turning their back on you. I learned that I was the one that left everyone behind when I made the decision to do wrong. I had a choice and I knew what the consequences could be.

The Streets Don't Love You Back

When you are in prison, life goes on and everything and everyone changes while you are gone.

When you are in prison everybody wants to know where you are from. Where I come from is not important to me. I did not give a damn where anyone was from. All I did was write letters to people back home. I was called "write man" from Detroit. Everyone told me they had never seen anyone write as much as I did.

In prison there are two things that brighten your day, the first is hearing your name called at mail time and the second is being called for a visit. The times that you don't hear your name called are tough.

One day I decided to go to the majors office to ask him if I qualify for the Honor Camp, he began to run my past by me, I thought that it didn't matter because it was thirteen years ago and I had stayed out of trouble for so long, but to him it was not good enough. I left his office feeling sick. I told myself that that I was still placing myself in Gods care and realized that his plan for me was different. I knew that God loved me and would open the gates for me one day as I was one of his best soldiers. When you get into the prison system, you are not a person you then become a number that is worth $38,000 to the prison.

There are rules in prison and the Golden rule in prison is keeping your eyes and ears open and your mouth shut, you will stay alive like that, however always be ready to put in work because it is a war zone. Trust no one in prison. Prison that's what it is. So when we do wrong we must ask ourselves is it really worth it? Are you willing to give up your freedom for prison life?

I believe that it's all about money in the prison system and people don't think that when you are in prison that you know what's going on in the streets. Once again it is all about who you know. I know many people in high and low places because

The Streets Don't Love You Back

I was never afraid of anyone in my life. The people, who really knew me, knew I would put in the work for what I believe in.

I knew of an inmate that was arrested for having 17 kilos of cocaine and he only received one year flat with no trial. Now how could that be? How did he walk away from that? Did he tell on someone else or did he pay the courts off? Think about it, one or the other. Ask yourself this, how do the drugs get out to the streets? They say they are trying to get the drugs off the streets but they are the ones putting it out there. They put it in our ghettos all across America. Sometimes I wonder if in the end is it all a trick, death or prison what do you think? There are those in high power and they get away with it for a moment, however when they are caught they will call their friends in high places to get them out of trouble because they owe them a favor.

It's all about who you know and how powerful they are that is the bottom line.

In prison I remember feeling as though time were standing still, or feeling as though I couldn't breathe in that place.

ON MY WAY HOME

I have always said it was a misunderstanding when it comes to be being locked up. Now it's almost over and I'm headed to the Parole Board to see if they are going to let me go home. I believe that God told those people to let his soldier out, as he has work to do. I was granted parole and I was released on February 17, 1994. Thanks to GOD almighty.

I got my stuff packed up and was ready for them to say "time to go". Little did I know I was going to a halfway house on Beekman where I had to stay, get a job and to prove myself.

I called my wife as soon as I hit the streets and told her where I was, but she had already called the prison and knew where I was. I hadn't seen her in so long I couldn't wait to see her. She came to see me and I found out that things weren't right. Her mother had passed away and she had been overwhelmed on her own she moved back to the ghetto and was living with another man. Like I said people change when you leave them. The situation was hard on me but I moved on and decided to concentrate on myself and get my life back together. I found a job at the Vernon Manor Hotel on Oak Street and met a lot of good people, Nate was one of them, and he turned out to be a real good friend all these years. While I was there I worked as a dishwasher then I got a second job at Days Inn on Central Parkway.

LIFE GETS BETTER

In 1995 I met some people who had an Internet business. They said that if I could get people to use their service they would hook me up with a website to sell my music so I got busy and that was when my website www.boydrec.com was created. They had put all the music that I created on that site, I continued my music career as I became a music producer, promoter and was released from the halfway house. In 1995 I was also released from parole. My life was looking better, good things were happening. I had started Boyd Records, Boyd Publishing and Boyd Films. I was soon approached by Jim Knippenberg from the Cincinnati Enquirer, he had heard about me from Buddy Gray who was a homeless activist who helped the homeless, only later to be killed by a homeless person. I had been involved in helping the homeless since being released from prison in 1994.

Boyd Records and P.C. a local musician had donated half the proceeds from the album called. "Make It Happen" to the Cincinnati Coalition for the Homeless in honor of slain activist Buddy Gray.

The Streets Don't Love You Back

I had corresponded with President Bill Clinton regarding the concerns of the homeless in America. To my surprise I received a letter of commendation and encouragement from President Bill Clinton.

I remember thinking to myself, I'm just a boy from the ghetto, I have gone through a lot in my life trying to find out who I am and always wanting to help others. Now here I am making my dream come true. I am currently the CEO and Founder of Boyd Records, Boyd Films, Boyd Publishing and Boyd Wear. Receiving this letter from the President of the United States was overwhelming and validated what I was doing. I thank God for bringing me to this point in my life and give him the glory.

MY HEART IS BROKEN

Later that year I received a devastating phone call from my mother. My mother told me that my oldest son who had gotten involved in the street life had killed someone. My heart was broken, but it was at that moment that I realized the heartache I had caused my mother in the past. I was just still in shock that my son had taken a life. He was a promising football player. He had played since he was a young boy, and scouts had been looking at him while he was in High School before he got into trouble. My son was only 18 and his life is destroyed because of the gang/street life. My heart was crushed.

The Streets Don't Love You Back

KEEP IT REAL

In 1998 I started the "Keep It Real Show". I had recently been a guest on a T.V. show called "In and around 452" hosted by Mr. Joe, who was interested in what I had been doing with the homeless and my music. After the show, he told me that I have a nice way of speaking and as we talked further we talked about me starting my own T.V. show. I had to take some classes in production and editing. After I received the Certification of Completion I was ready to get started.
The Keep It real Show was born. The focus of the show was on interviewing music artists and playing music videos. It gave me another way to reach out to others. I have had many guests on my show including: Silk, Ginuwine, Club Nouveau, Ronnie Laws, Men at Large, Heat Wave, The Manhattans, The Lox, Ball, MJG, Twista, 112, Mystikal and many more.
The Keep It Real Show continues today and is also moving forward with —Keep It Real Political.
I thank Way Cross and Media Bridges for airing my show all these years.

REUNITED WITH FATHER

On February 3, 2008 I met my father for the first time again after many years. He is now in a long term care facility. For the past 30 years I had only seen him on T.V. or listened to him on the radio. Dad started to cry and said, "My son is here". I cried because for the first time in my life I have the chance to tell my father how much he hurt me when I was a child and for not being a part of my life. He told me that one of his biggest regrets in life was not being in my life and doing for me.

53

The Streets Don't Love You Back

I told my Father —you missed all the years that I played sports, I can sing, produce music, write, I'm a good business man and I have been good at all that I do. When I was young Mom used to ask you to come and see me and you never came and as a child that destroyed me and the dreams that I had. I was only nine years old when I witnessed my stepfather's murder and I needed you more than ever and you weren't there.

I had no man in my life to show me the way and that is why I turned to the brother's on the street. You never gave me a penny, a pair of shoes, a baseball, a football, you never gave mom child support to feed us and she had to work multiple jobs to care for us. You once told me that you would help me with my music career and you never did. Dad I lived a very hard life and on the streets trying to make a living while you were living the good life. I have always played life like a chess game. You always have to be moving in the right direction because being in check mate means the game is over.

My Father is now 72, has multiple medical problems and suffered a stroke. At the time I visited my father he was on hospice care. I was able to visit with my father and find out more about him after all I am Robert D. Boyd Jr. I was able to sit face to face on multiple visits and confront my father with the deep pain and hurt that I had carried all these years. My father was an upstanding man, a Reverend with his own congregation and an Author of 64 books. I asked my father, "How can you say that you are a man of God when you had children that you had forsaken", when God says, I will never forsake you. I told my father —I know that God carried me through all the hard times in my life and that I am the man I am today because he did not forsake me. God has greater things for me to do here on this earth. As my father and I sat and shared, with tears in our eyes he told me he was truly sorry for not being a father to me. I said,

The Streets Don't Love You Back

"Pops I forgive you and I wish you peace forever. I applaud you for following your dreams and making them a reality and I plan to do the same". I am my Fathers son.

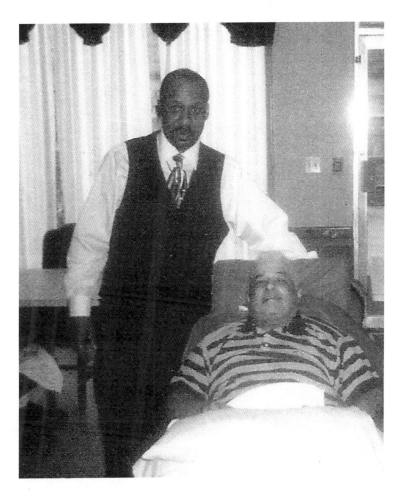

Robert Boyd Jr. and father Robert Boyd Sr. 2008

I am a motivational Speaker and the CEO/Founder of The Streets Don't Love You Back Movement. A movement that strives to educate our youth about the dangers of gang violence and drugs and that there are many alternatives to the gang/thug life.

If you are in a gang or dealing with drugs you are setting yourself up to fail. Living that kind of life will ruin your relationships and hurt your loved ones.

Living the gang/thug life leaves you with only two choices and in the end you will either be dead or spend the rest of your life in prison.

Like I said, I ran with some of the most dangerous men in the Eastside of Detroit for many years. Most of my friends, cousins and acquaintances are dead or serving life in Prison. I live today, not because I was lucky but because I was blessed. God had a better plan for me than I did for myself and when I began to listen to him, my life started changing. I got away from the streets, and all those around me who had any influence over me. I had to move away from it all and start over which was not an easy thing to do.

A wise man learns and a weak man falls because he never learns.

God never leaves us. We leave God when we choose to make the wrong decisions in our life. Some of us think that we can do it by ourselves or that we don't need anyone or anything else to succeed in life, that we can do it on our own. However, that is where we fool ourselves and get caught up in the game. Open your heart to God and his blessings and your life will change just as mine did.

I am sharing my life story so that I can reach out and help those who are in need of change. I have founded the Streets Don't Love You Back Movement in order to educate our youth in America from cities to rural areas that violence and drugs are not the answer and the streets don't love you back. It is time to stop the violence, heal the anger pain and hurt. Put God first in your life, your family second and you will truly be blessed.

The Streets Don't Love You Back

This is for all my "Homies" and for all the senseless deaths of innocent people caused from gang violence and drugs.

REST IN PEACE

Darryl "Dijon" Jackson
Larry "Fab' Thompson
"Maserati", Richard Earl Carter
Steven Washington
Demetrius Holloway
Gary Charles Hunter
Douglas Kenneth Stewart, Jr.
Antonio Cortez Corbin
Dwight Raymond Soloman
Terrance "Boogaloo" Brown
Scott Taylor
Darryl Kidd
Michael Trice Kenny M.
Charles Rucker
Twitt
Black Mike Junebug
Darin Topps
Warren

The Streets Don't Love You Back

TERRANCE BROWN
BEST FRIENDS LEADER
1985-1993

The youngest of the four Brown brothers, Terrance Boogaloo Brown followed in the steps of his notorious older brothers by joining them in their quest for street fame, riches and the elimination of their foes. Terrance found himself in charge of the gang's enforcement wing following the murders of Ezra and Gregory in December of 1986 and the incarceration of family leader Reggie shortly thereafter.

Terrance wasted no time in establishing himself a reputation for violence worthy of the Brown name in the often brutal streets of Detroit with the murder of James Lamont on March 16, 1989. The then twenty year old Terrance received a death sentence for encroaching on Best Friends territory and going so far as to raid the gangs membership to beef up his own organization following the death of Maserati Rick Carter five months before.

With older brother in prison sentenced to life for the murder of Steve Roussell, Boogaloo orchestrated and then carried out Lamont's murder outside of the Regis Hotel. The brazen attack placed Terrance Brown atop the wish list for every law enforcement officer and task force member in Detroit. Prior to the Lamont shooting Terrance Brown had a clean arrest record in spite of his entanglement in the complicated affairs surrounding the transition of Best Friends leadership in 1988-89.

For more than a year Terrance Brown frustrated the efforts of law enforcement officials looking to nab him for his murderous deeds. Terrance quickly became one of the most sought after criminals in the motor city after a rash of shootings connected with Best Friends raked the city. News articles tracking the death toll ran weekly recounting the latest shootout or unidentified body found in an alleyway or side street. Terrance turned himself in and was eventually tried and acquitted in the Lamont murder and returned to the side of his brother Reggie who had emerged from prison after having a previous murder conviction overturned and was released in February of 1992 on bond.

Reggie's freedom should have been short lived as the bond was revoked the following month but the gang leader disappeared along with his brother and several close associates. As authorities looked high and low for the murderous pair, Reggie Brown proved his violent reputation was well deserved when he was spotted three months later on Buckingham Street.

The notoriety of Brown made him an easily recognizable figure especially within the Best Friends territory and he made no effort to conceal his identity as he walked up to the home of Alfred Austin exchanging pleasantries along the way with neighbors moments before opening fire on Austin and two other people standing nearby. Once the barrage had ceased, Alfred Austin —an associate of Terrance Brown was facing weapons charges in Kentucky and was rumored to be considering a plea deal with prosecutors looking to build airtight case against the Browns, was the first to fall, Harry Roper and Lawrence Gainey were targeted because they were potential witnesses to the attack.

The final victim was three year old Lori Roper the daughter of Harry who was hit by a stray bullet. Five days later a new warrant was issued by Magistrate Richard Halloran Jr. of the thirty sixth District Court charges Reginald Brown with four counts of murder in the first degree. Both Brown brothers fled Detroit and took refuge in New York where they were spotted in June of 1993. The notorious Reginald Brown was taken into custody along with William Wilkes, another wanted criminal, as he attempted to enter a car. His brother Terrance was spotted in the area but made an escape by disappearing into a subway tunnel.

With the possible life sentence hanging in the balance, Terrance Boogaloo brown continued to operate within the drug world securing $600,000 in cash from his attorney Paul Curtis to transact a drug purchase in Atlanta Georgia in August of 1993.

The last remaining member of the notorious Brown family which left such a lasting impression on Detroit's Eastside was found wrapped in a plastic bag and a bed sheet with masking tape in the back of a stolen pickup truck in the parking lot of the Ramada Renaissance Hotel in College park, Georgia. Brown had been shot once in the head at an undisclosed location and transported to the parking lot by a man caught on the hotels security camera. The man was then joined by another man and the duo escaped undetected in another vehicle. Terrance Brown's body lay unidentified in an Atlanta morgue for nearly a week before authorities were able to place an identity on him. The case remains unsolved and the only

The Streets Don't Love You Back

information released by investigators was that Brown had been wearing only his underwear and a black T-shirt. Terrance Brown was only 25 years old when he was murdered but lived a life filled with violence and grief.

The Streets Don't Love You Back

REGINALD BROWN
BEST FRIENDS ENFORCEMENT CHIEF
1986-1989

Burly and intimidating was the way Reggie Brown was once described calculating, cold and unforgiving are terms which also apply to this once powerful leader of an eastside drug gang responsible for countless deaths during the mid to late 80's. While Reggie Brown did not create Best Friends, it was his deeds that led to the organizations fierce reputation on the bloody streets of Detroit. While
Best Friends was a drug gang headed by Richard "Maserati Rick" Carter and his best friend Demetrius Holloway, Reggie rose to prominence as the leader of the gang's enforcement arm known as the wrecking crew. Best Friends was formed by legendary drug dealer Maserati Rick Carter in 1985 after a series of battles with rival drug dealers cut into his ability to concentrate specifically on business.

The Streets Don't Love You Back

In an effort to rectify this situation, Carter approached Reggie —a man known for his propensity for violence, with an offer of protection. Carter would finance the formation of a security team in which Brown would direct it's movements on behalf of Best friend's drug wing. Brown agreed and began recruiting a crack of shooters who were outfitted with high powered assault rifles, automatic pistols, body armor and bullet proof vests paid for courtesy of Carter, Holloway and teenage drug sensation White Boy Rick Wershe.

Reggie's recruiting efforts started close to home where he counted his three brothers Ezra, Gregory "Ghost" and Terrance "Boogaloo" as his closest aides.

Up to this point Reggie was the only one of the Brown brothers known as a potential threat to do great bodily harm with the others picking up arrest on relatively sedate charges like auto theft and possession of marijuana with the intent to distribute.

All of that would change in short order as the Browns took up arms on behalf of Best Friends defending the gang's territory with a vicious fervor which met the approval of their flashy financier Maserati Rick. With Reggie leading the Charge, Best Friends fortunes soared and soon were regarded among the elite traffickers in Michigan along with organizations headed by the Davis Family, Young Boys and the Chambers.

Less than a year after it was founded, the wrecking crew was the most feared enforcement arm in the Detroit underworld taking on support groups like Pony Down and small but well run operations by former clients of Carter's like Big Ed Hanserd and James Lamont.

During the course of these battles, allies were lost but none closer or more devastating to Reggie than the loss of his two younger brothers Ezra and Gregory within a week of one another in December of 1986. The death of Ezra and Gregory did nothing to deter the two remaining brothers from

The Streets Don't Love You Back

continuing along the path of violence which had caused their loss but instead seemed to light a fire which would rage out of control for the next seven years. Reggie was tried and acquitted for the September 1986 murder of nineteen year old Carlton Journey and the wounding of Pamela Brown. Investigators also named him as the prime suspect in the shooting of William Miles in May of 1987. This attack also claimed the life of Kirk Levy a 25 year old member of a rival gang. Rockin Reggie was acquitted of all charges in relation to this shooting as well.

With all of the attention brought on by a rash of killings, Reggie continued his horrid rampage killing an associate of White Boy Rick Wershe a teenage kingpin after a business dispute.

No friends or associates were exempt from retribution when Reggie Brown's wrath was incurred. This lesson was demonstrated in the case of Steve Roussell who was a close friend of white Boy Rick Wershe and was at the very least familiar with Reggie Brown and his reputation. Roussell and Brown had a disagreement during a cocaine deal which led to Brown administering a vicious beating upon Roussell.

This altercation led to brown being placed on probation. Unsatisfied with the results of the altercation, Reggie struck once more in the early morning hours of September 12, 1987 in a house in the 13600 block of Glennwood. Brown according to statements given by Patrick McCloud shot and killed Roussell as he slept in the home owned by Rick Wershe Jr. According to McCloud he was sleeping in the living room when he was awakened by the sound of gunfire and saw Reggie shooting Roussell.

McCloud was himself shot in the back as he attempted to flee the room. Brown was arrested, tried and later convicted April 29, 1988 of second degree murder for the Roussell shooting. The jury needed only two and a half hours to reach a decision.

The Streets Don't Love You Back

The exact cause of the second rift between Roussell and Brown has not been determined but it can only summed up that the money was not the issue as officers called to the scene of the shooting found a safe filled with $30,000 in cash in a room on the second floor. Authorities believed they had rid themselves of Reggie Brown when he was sentenced to life in prison on May 20, 1998. The life sentence imposed on Reggie Brown robbed best Friends of their most intimidating enforcer and signaled a weakening of the once mighty organization to its competition. Just four months after Reggie was shipped away, Maserati Rick was struck down as he lay recovering from a previous attempt on his life in Mt. Carmel Mercy Hospital on September 12, 1988. Carter had been engaged in an open warfare with an upstart dealer known as Big Ed. Edward Hanserd emerged victorious from the fray with the successful elimination of the flashy Carter.

Reggie Brown made a shocking return when he managed to have his murder conviction overturned on appeal in February of 1989. Released on bond my Magistrate George Crockett III, Brown returned to the streets intent on establishing himself in an increased capacity in Detroit's drug world. Reggie's operation had continued to operate under the direction of his younger brother

Terrance who had himself undergone a transformation and was now feared almost as much as his older brother. Reggie wasted no time in declaring the wrecking crew independent of the remains of Best Friends.

While he remained on good terms with Demetrius Holloway the new leader of Best friends, Reggie sought desperately to carve himself a larger piece of the pie dominated by organizations like the Chambers Brothers, DFG and his own Best Friends. An increase in violence between Best Friends and other groups trying to administer the knockout blow caused an uproar among law enforcement agencies and officials who attributed the influx in violence to

Brown's return to action. Reggie's bond was quickly revoked but he disappeared before authorities could locate him. While on the lam, Reggie struck against one of his own who was considering a prosecution deal against his younger brother. Alfred Austin was a member of Reggies, revitalized Wrecking Crew participation in the gang's expansion efforts. Austin had recently been charged with federal weapons violations in Kentucky. Authorities offered him a plea deal in exchange for information against Terrance Brown in what has been described as a misguided show of loyalty. Austin told one of the Brown's about the offer and returned to the gang's fold in good graces. Or so he thought.

On Saturday May 9th, fugitive Reginald Brown walked up to a home on Buckingham street exchanging greetings with several people before opening fire on Austin as he sat conversing with two other men on the porch of his home. Brown then turned his pistol on 24 year old Harry Roper and 23 Year old Lawrence Gainey. During the shooting 3 year old Lori Roper was struck and killed by a stray bullet. George Ward assistant to the Wayne County prosecutor announced —we want him pretty bad... there are four people dead, we are talking about mass murder here. While no volunteered information outside of those wounded in Brown's previous rampages, the death of 3 year old Lori Roper brought several witnesses to come forward and identify Brown as the perpetrator of the attack.

An arrest warrant signed by Magistrate Richard Halloran of the 36th District Court was issued Thursday May 14, 1992 charging Brown with four counts of 1st degree murder. It would take investigators 13 months to locate the fugitive, but Reginald Brown was taken into custody as he attempted to get in to a car in Manhattan. Authorities also spotted his brother Terrance who was wanted on a separate murder charge, but were unsuccessful in apprehending him after a motorcycle chase which included Brown striking a pedestrian before escaping into a subway tunnel.

Reggie was returned to Detroit where he faced a possible death sentence for the four murders.

The death sentence was dropped by the prosecutor's office but Brown was convicted and sentenced this time to serve four life sentences in prison. Reggie Brown remains incarcerated and his younger brother Terrance was killed in a drug deal gone badly less than two months after Reggie was apprehended.

Best Friends decimated by death and the efforts of law enforcement, was eventually elbowed aside with Brown and Wershe serving life sentences, Boogaloo Brown, Maserati Rick carter and Demetrius Holloway all murdered in the street, best Friends is no longer considered an active force in Detroit's drug trade.

The Streets Don't Love You Back

RICHARD WERSHE JR.
(White Boy Rick)
1985-1990

 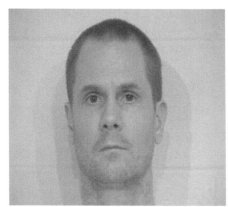

Very rarely does a teenager attract the attention Richard Wershe Jr., garnered during his heyday in Detroit. Wershe's star rose like the sun lighting up the dark allies and backstreets on the eastside of Detroit where he played his trade. By all accounts Wershe's prominence lasted little more than four years before he was caught and sentenced to life in prison under Michigan's stringent drug laws. Richard Wershe Jr., was born April 15, 1969 to Richard and Darlene Wershe. The Wershe family included one other addition a daughter Dawn born three years earlier.

The Wershe children were raised by their father after their parents divorced in 1975. Richard Sr. owned and a string of businesses including a Colorado based firm that manufactured weapons parts in addition to a second satellite installation business which would in inadvertently lead

The Streets Don't Love You Back

Richard Jr., into a life of crime and drugs. Richard Jr., met Johnny Curry the leader of a notorious crack ring when he accompanied his father to install a satellite television system in Curry's home. Shortly thereafter young Richard began running errands for the Curry organization quickly advancing from running errands to delivering narcotics. Wershe apparently impressed the leader of the Curry gang who took Richard under his wing and shared with the youngster the tricks of the drug trade. Wershe put the lessons he learned to good use when Johnny Curry and 6 of his workers were charged with operating a multimillion dollar cocaine operation on the eastside of Detroit. The breakup of the Curry ring was lauded in the Detroit press as a major blow against the flow of drugs decimating the inner city communities during the 80's. With the removal of his mentor, a 16 year old Wershe began an unlikely climb through the eastside drug trade branching out on his own. By the time Johnny Curry stood in recorders court and received a twenty-year sentence for running what was alleged to be one of Detroit's most profitable drug rings, his former student was well on his way to surpassing the accomplishments of the professor. In spite of his age, race and appearance, Richard Wershe won the respect of some of the most notorious figures to operate within the Detroit city limits at a time when the city was recognized as one of the most violent metro areas in the country. Wershe formed an alliance with Best Friends leaders Richard Carter, Demetrius Holloway and Reginald Brown which afforded him the protection of the most formidable protection crew in Detroit. Best Friends started out as a collaboration of Richard Carter and his best friend Demetrius Holloway in the drug business. Best Friends gained influence and power following the demise of several larger gangs like Young Boys Inc., the Curry organization and the DFG "The Davis Family Gang," in a highly publicized assault by local and federal law enforcement agencies resulting in a string of convictions starting in the early 80's. As Best Friends finances increased, Carter decided to finance the organization of an enforcement arm headed up by the Brown brothers.

The enforcement arm gained notoriety under the name of the wrecking crew during the mid-80's as they fought off the efforts of rival groups to infringe upon Carter and Holloway's territory. The association with Best Friends served to further the career and reputation of Wershe who then became an important supplier of the gang's cocaine and marijuana.

Wershe fortunes soared as his dealings with Best Friends afforded him the type of lifestyle dreamed about by those he had shared a classroom with just a few years before. While other kids his age made plans to save enough money to rent a limo for the prom, Wershe purchased a new Mercedes Benz. While other kids worked in malls for minimum wage, Wershe pulled in $100,000 a week from his drug operation. The slightly built young man with the chubby cheeks and blond hair made his mark as an adolescent in a career field that claimed the lives of bigger, tougher and more experienced men every day. Luck just seemed to be on this young man's side that is until a string of highly publicized arrests, brought the dream crashing down at his feet. Wershe's rise in the drug trade coincided with the addition of his sister Dawn who drifted in and out of treatment centers, clinics and intervention programs. White Boy Rick's string of good luck came to an end in September of 1986 when a DEA agent was successful in making two small purchases of cocaine at the Wershe home. The buys were used to secure warrants for at least two subsequent raids on the Wershe home but resulted in no charges being filed against White Boy Rick.

Wershe Jr., became a primary target of DEA surveillance teams in November 1986 when the 17 year old was picked up along with two friends at Metro Airport as the trio returned from a trip to Miami. One of Wershe's companions drew a six year prison term for drug trafficking but the juvenile Wershe skipped free without any charges being logged against him. Four months later authorities charged Rick with possession after an amount found to be less than fifty grams of cocaine was found in a Hayes street home in which he was visiting. Two months later members of the Detroit Police Department stopped him near his home on Hampshire. Rick was charged with intent to deliver cocaine. This was a highly controversial charge as the officers had located a box containing 9 lbs. of cocaine buried in a yard next door to the Wershe family home.

The suddenly star crossed Wershe Jr., was arrested yet again on October 13, 1987 when he and Robert Poulack were arrested following a traffic stop on Manistique. The officers who searched the car the pair was driving found 11 lbs., of cocaine. Wershe spent 7 days in jail before winning his release by posting a bond of $100,000 on October 21. Facing a life sentence for drug dealing, Wershe managed to anger his defense team when his January court appearance was overrun by a mob of his young drug dealing associates who packed the hall ways of the courthouse. The crowd which consisted of young men and women around Wershe's age, made quite a scene. Defended by two of Detroit's finest criminal defense attorney's, Wershe showed up for his second bond hearing dressed in a double breasted Armani suit while the hallways of the court overflowed with youngsters carrying large wads of cash dressed in sweat suites adorned with beepers and thick gold chains. Freed after posting a cash bond of $200,000 White Boy Rick was released yet again to an elated crowd who avoided the glare of the lights and cameras of news crews and media shows like 60 minutes who showed up to film Detroit's latest criminal sensation.

The Streets Don't Love You Back

SYLVESTOR MURRAY
DRUG SUPPLIER
1978-1993

After spending much of his adult life as a shadowy participant in many of Detroit's as one of the main targets of a federal indictment aimed at the leadership of the notorious Young Boys Inc., drug gang which dominated the streets of Detroit for nearly five years until the December 1982 indictment came down. At the time of the indictment, Young Boys was responsible for an estimated 25 to 30% of Detroit's drug traffic.

This equated to sales of $7,500,000 a week for the pioneering group. Investigators lauded the December 7th capture of Seal as a major blow to the organization as he was the gang's primary supplier and a key link between Young Boys and the Davis Family who were responsible for securing the product through their international contacts.

The Streets Don't Love You Back

During the height of the Young Boys operation, Seal provided the gang with 3 kilos of pure heroin a week at a cost of $600,000. Y.B.I. operatives then would dilute the heroin down to purity levels of 2to 3% and then sell the product in $8 to $10 bags. During his bond hearing evidence was provided which showed an encounter in which Seal passed a package of heroin to an undercover narcotics agent that later tested 52% pure. Authorities began targeting the fruits of Murray's labor seizing at least $1,300,000 in cash from the drug lord during the course of several raids aimed at breaking down his and Y.B.I's influence in Detroit's drug circles.

During one raid on an apartment at the Jeffersonian (located at 900 E. Jefferson) more than $700,000 in cash sitting in brown paper bags was confiscated. Seemingly unfazed by the loss of such a large amount of cash, Murray told one of the raiding officers that his safe contained another $80,000 but he hadn't opened it in so long he no longer remembered the combination. Another of Murray's associates was not so casual and attempted to escape the raiding party by leaping from balcony to balcony 27 floors above ground before breaking into a woman's apartment where he proceeded to phone his attorney before being taken into custody.

Sylvester Murray was born and raised in Detroit and conducted his first transaction within the drug business as a 14 year old. While his name was well known on the street, one of Detroit's social workers admitted to hearing the name Seal in connection with the narcotics trafficking as far back as 1969, Murray would remain an unknown for another decade. During this time the enterprising
Murray from Detroit's Northwestern high with respectable marks and a reputation as a quiet seemingly shy loner.

Throughout the 70's Murray would work closely with members of the DFG "Davis Family Gang", a group of brothers who would play prominently in the future growth of

The Streets Don't Love You Back

the heroin business in black areas of Detroit. Many people familiar with Murray admitted knowing of his success but attributed it to a sting of businesses he had run or financed. While his demeanor was always quiet, polite and respectable, Seal had an affinity for nice things. He was often spotted riding about town in one of the many fine autos he owned which included a new Mercedes Benz, Cadillac and a custom convertible Corvette.

Sylvester Murray legitimate businessman owned an endless number of neatly tailored suites while his alter ego Seal was spotted at Y.B.I. parties wearing suite suites accented with lots of gold. While Sylvester Murray was undoubtedly a fine businessman, his underworld nature often shined through in legitimate dealings such as the time he sought to purchase a new home.

Murray took a liking to a home located in the 24000 block of Manistee in Oak Park, Michigan. Murray reportedly approached the owners with a suitcase full of cash one night and made an offer to buy the house which until that moment wasn't on the market. Eventually a deal was worked out but the seller insisted on being paid with a check as opposed to cash in a suite case.

Murray also owned a home in the 19000 block of Nadol in Southfield, Michigan which he shared with Darlene Davis, a woman who identified herself to officers arriving to investigate a call of a domestic dispute in 1981. Although no charges were filed, officers did confiscate a loaded .357 magnum and an unloaded .37 caliber pistol both of which Seal admitted to owning. Prior to this run-in with authorities, Murray's record showed arrests for carrying concealed weapons and a controlled substance.

The result of these cases is unknown but they had no bearing on the fact that Seal was in possession of a loaded firearm. When Murray learned of the pending federal indictment against Young Boys, an associate claimed that

The Streets Don't Love You Back

Murray began to worry about the fleet of cars which were being purchased in the names of many of his love interests which were on welfare.

As Seal's drug business expanded, his quest to fulfill the orders of his clientele called for him to travel extensively to cities around the country. On one wiretap Murray is heard in a phone conversation detailing to an associate, I had to stop in Chicago for a couple of days... I left tonight. I'm supposed to be in Los Angeles., man, but I had to wait on some people. Authorities say these trips were drug runs and argued during his trial that he had once made a trip to L.A. to secure a shipment of 4lbs. of brown heroin from Mexico.

At his bail hearing the court ordered him held on a $10,000,000 bond while several of his co-defendants received virtually no bond at all. Murray was remanded immediately into federal custody and shipped to the federal penitentiary in Milan, Michigan pending trial. Friday June 3, 1983 marked the end of the line for Seal Murray who had emerged from the Young Boys federal indictment as one of the most notorious drug traffickers in Detroit after spending more than a decade as a relatively unknown figure. Convicted of drug conspiracy charges, the then 30 year old Murray accepted the jury's decision after 3 days of deliberation. Also found guilty in the case were two Murray associates Michael Jenkins and Velma Bailes whom authorities claimed stashed cash and drugs for Seal in their home. All three were sentenced August 3, 1983 with Murray receiving the harshest treatment drawing a term of fifteen years and a $100,000 fine.

Two days after being convicted on drug conspiracy charges, the government attacked Murray's personal holdings seizing five buildings including an apartment complex and four single family homes. The feds also had their eyes on the $1.3 million in cash seized from Murray and his associates but Seal's attorney claimed the money was the proceeds of Murray's legitimate enterprises which included a party store and a car wash in addition to his role of an auto trader and real estate broker.

Murray emerged from prison in August of 1991 after serving 8 years of the 15 year sentence and promptly returned to the drug business setting up another high profile organization which was toppled with his arrest in November of 1993.

Murray along with his wife Darlene (mentioned as Darlene Davis) and 9 other associates were picked up after four raids on locations which included a home in the 19000 block of Nadol in Southfield which had been seizure list following the original conviction. At the time of his arrest, Murray stood charged with money laundering, heroin and cocaine trafficking. Agents seized an additional $160,000 in cash, 6 vehicles and 3lbs. of heroin.

The Streets Don't Love You Back

YOUNG BOYS INCORPORATED – Y.B.I.

RAYMOND PEOPLES   DWAYNE DAVIS .W.

Y.B.I. was among the first African-American drug cartels that operated on street corners. They controlled about 40% of the heroin traffic in Detroit, Michigan from the summer of 1978 through the late 1980's. It is alleged that at the height of their reign, the Y.B.I's drug business was making more money than the nearly bankrupted Chrysler Corporation. The group was formed by a small group of neighborhood friends in 1977. In the beginning, all of the boys were in their late teens. Dwayne Davis (a.k.a. Wonderful Wayne or W.W.), and Raymond Peoples were two of the founders who became bosses. A few years later Butch Jones, (a.k.a. Big Boy) was paroled from prison and joined the organization. It was about this time that Y.B.I. split into three separate crews (W.W., Big Boy and Raymond). From the start, YBI's main place of operation was the Dexter/Davison neighborhood on Detroit's west side. About two years after its formation, Y.B.I. completely took over the heroin trade in and around Detroit with sales estimated at about $300,000 per day. After the split, W.W. sent one of his top lieutenants to Boston to expand his operation. About a year after being in Boston, the crew he took to Boston with him, along with new members from Boston, took over most of that city's heroin trade. Sales peaked at about $50,000 per day.

The organization in Detroit was seriously crippled in 1982, when in September of that year, it was alleged that Butch Jones ordered the execution of W.W. because of a turf dispute. W.W. was gunned down on the corner of Columbus and Lawton on Detroit's west side. A few months later, on December 7, Raymond Peoples, Butch Jones and 41 of Y.B.I.'s top Lieutenants were indicted, convicted, and later sentenced to long prison terms. Most people believed that because of W.W.'s death none of his crew was indicted. After Raymond Peoples was released from prison he was shot to death as he sat in a car on the city's west side. The lieutenant that —W.W. sent to Boston came back to Detroit after W.W.'s death and took over what was left of Y.B.I. He operated for about another six years, taking the group to another level until crack cocaine became the drug of choice over heroin. One of his soldiers who came back from Boston with him was Steven Sealy. Sealy is best known for being gunned down and killed as he sat in Whitney Houston's Rolls Royce in front of a Boston club. In the car with him was his future brother in law, Bobby Brown. Butch Jones was released after serving 12 years in federal prison, but was eventually indicted again on drug and murder charges. Under US Federal Law, anyone who is convicted of a drug related murder is eligible for the death penalty. Facing such punishment, Jones cooperated with federal authorities for a lesser sentence.

The Streets Don't Love You Back

Y.B.I. was the model upon which later figures like the Chambers Brothers, Best Friends and more recently Clifford Jones used to set up their own successful organizations. Founded on Detroit's Westside in 1978 by Milton "Butch" Jones, Raymond Peoples and Mark Marshall, Y.B.I. at the peak of its strength could call on the services of 300 members or associates to enforce its leaders will in gang circles.

Supplied with their product by businessman/pusher Seal Murray, Y.B.I. used school aged children to push their product which carried colorful street labels such as Atomic Dog, Whip Cracker, Rolls Royce and Freak of the Week.

The gang rewarded hard working salesman, women and children with gifts that included expensive jewelry, leather coats, diamonds, concert tickets and bicycles. In testimony presented to the US senate, authorities stated that Y.B.I. gained control of the street level distribution of narcotics in the city of Detroit a few months after the gang's organization on the playground of Birney Elementary School the Monterey-Dexter neighborhood of Detroit. The gang's terrorizing hold over the narcotics industry came to a halt with the arrest and conviction of dozens of leaders including Butch Jones, the enforcer and founder of the notorious A-Team enforcement squad who directed his troops from the business end of a gold plated pistol. Mark Marshall, Raymond Peoples, a man with a reputation for violence and their supplier and advisor Sylvester Seal Murray.

By the mid 90's many of the big names, Cary Goins, Charles Obey and Kirk McGurt associated with Y.B.I. were dead or in Prison but their legacy was carrying on through the success of drug gangs making a name for themselves on the Eastside of Detroit. Butch made an ill-fated attempt to regain his place atop Detroit's drug world resulting in a possible death sentence. His latest scheme led to the indictment of his wife Portia and several other people including a former Detroit political figure.

The Streets Don't Love You Back

Maurice MoHeart Gibbs
(Butch Jones Cousin)

Curtis Napier, a.k.a.
Kurk GcGurk

The Streets Don't Love You Back

MILTON DAVID JONES "Butch" Y. B. I.

At the age of fourteen Milton David Jones was introduced to the world of drug dealing by his brother-in-law who he referred to as a master operator. Initially Jones sold small amounts of heroin while serving as a security guard and lookout during transactions.

Jones claims to have killed for the first time at the age of 15. By his own account, Butch Jones shot and killed a suspected stick up man at a dope house on Duane. In the incident Jones reportedly recognized a man who accompanied a woman who came to the house to buy some dope as the infamous "stick-up" Mike. Jones quickly deduced that Mike had come to the dope house to rob it and ultimately kill everyone there so he opened the front door and without warning shot the suspected bandit with a twelve gauge shotgun as he stood out in the yard. Following this cold hearted murder Jones claims that he became a feared and respected member of the underworld culture. The murder caused the dope spot to be shut down for a time but when it opened back up, it was under the control of the fifteen year old Jones. While moving into the heroin business, Jones began making the rounds of all of the seedy nightspots meeting old time hustlers, gamblers, pimps and peddlers.

At such a tender age Jones claims to have acquired his "PhD from the streets." With his street reputation firmly established Jones admits to participating in paid hits, robberies and arson. While in the process of completely terrorizing all who came in contact with the infamous Butch Jones, he made his first mistake by killing a man who he suspected of participating in the robbery of a friend of his at a local drug spot. Jones and two others were picked up and charged with murder on January 17, 1974.

While sitting in jail awaiting the determination of his future, Milton suffered the loss of one of his brothers who was killed during the commission of a robbery. On the same day, his girlfriend and later wife Portia Sturtevant gave birth to his son Jamaky. Jones was sentenced to a seven year term in March of 1975 after taking a plea deal for manslaughter for his role in the killing. Jones served his time in Jackson and later Iona Reformatory before earning his release in 1978.

Within a month of his return to the streets of Detroit, Milton Jones, Mark Marshall and Raymond Peoples organized Young Boys Inc, Young Boys Inc., started off as a small insignificant band of drug peddlers operating out of Detroit's Monterey Dexter Eastside neighborhood. Initially all shots were called by 25 year old Mark Marshall with assistance from Raymond Peoples. Control of the gang was passed onto Peoples and Milton David Jones in 1979 when Marshall fled the motor city in favor of California by way of Mississippi.

The Streets Don't Love You Back

Jones and Peoples had taken their marching orders from the older more experienced Marshall but came together in transforming Young Boys Inc., into a multi-million dollar organized crime syndicate.

This transformation was plotted and ruthlessly carried out under the guidance of Butch Jones. Young Boys fortunes soared when Jones turned to Seal Murray to supply his operation with heroin and cocaine smuggled into the country from various points around the globe by international smuggler and financier Reginald Davis. Murray used his connections to members of the Davis Family Gang to secure large shipments of narcotics which were then distributed to members of Young Boys Inc. Jones began using his reputation as a killer to recruit a core of young preteen salesmen who would out of a combination of fear and respect for the older more experienced criminal were willing to demonstrate their loyalty by enforcing the edicts of their leader through an unprecedented show of brutality.

As YBI's fortunes soared, so did the murder rate among young black males in Detroit. Jones enforced a strict code of discipline among his troops calling for all dope to be turned in to a designated spot by 6 pm. If the dope was returned late or short, the offender could expect a beating at the hands of Jones or a member of his security force known as the wrecking crew.

Jones relied heavily on a trusted team of lieutenants to look out for the interests of YBI while he enjoyed the fruits of their labor.

Jones bought a string of homes in and around Detroit which he used to stay one step ahead of law enforcement officials and rival traffickers alike. Much like Seal Murray, Butch developed an affinity for fast cars and easy women. The collaboration of Murray and Jones proved to be a hard combination to beat for smaller groups such as Pony Down headed by Leroy Buttrom Willis. Murray's contacts with the Davis Family kept Young

The Streets Don't Love You Back

Boys Inc., supplied with the entire heroin they needed in the beginning but later Jones would use his womanizing skills to forge an alliance with dealers operating out of New York.

By 1983 Young Boys street sales were estimated in the neighborhood of $400 million dollars annually. At the top sat Milton David Jones, a man with little formal education running a criminal empire which rivaled the biggest legitimate companies. As the fortune and reputation of Young Boys Inc., expanded so did the desire of federal officials to see the largest dope ring in Michigan smashed.

Authorities closed in raiding several Young Boys strong holds harassing the group's street level workers and lieutenants. During one such raid, officers arrested a 19 year old member of the gang draped in gold with an estimated value which exceeded $100,000. It was during the early stages of these raids that 17 year old Carey Vincent Goins opened fire on two undercover narcotics officers killing William Green leaving his 36 year old partner suffering from a shoulder wound. Goins was quickly apprehended and convicted on a charge of murder but Mayor Coleman Young initiated a plan which eventually led to the dismantling of the Jones Empire.

The second phase of the attack then netted authorities, two million dollars' worth of cocaine and $800,000 in cash. The raid was conducted on May 18th at the Jeffersonian Apartments. This move was followed by a second highly publicized raid on a home which turned out to be a stash spot for Seal Murray's cash. This deprived the operation of another $633,000 in operating capitol. One more major seizure resulted in the loss of 2,200 packets of product already packaged for distribution. The constant pressure began to take its toll on the rings members as Seal Murray became increasingly paranoid by the frequency with which he had been hit for large sums of cash and dope. Butch Jones on the other hand hadn't seemed phased by the turn of events and continued to maintain a high profile in his usual areas. With the feds closing in on their base of operations, Young Boys made a push into other markets and soon controlled heroin trafficking in Pontiac and Flint, Michigan as well.

The success of the drug business provided plenty opportunity for jealousy to developed between Butch and members of the ring. Soon splinter groups began forming including one headed by Dewayne Davis, a man said to have been a friend of Butch Jones before money caused a rift between them.

Dewayne Davis a.k.a. "Wonderful Wayne" broke away from Young Boys and started his own crew known as H2O. In an effort to establish a profitable base of operations, Davis made the mistake of trying to muscle in on a Young Boys spot near Lawton.

The spot belonged to Curtis Napier known as Kurt McGurk on the street. Napier was one of Butch Jones top lieutenants and a feared hothead with a quick trigger. When Davis showed up on Lawton with a plan to sell his own brand of heroin, Napier approached him and asked if he had gotten Jones permission to sell his own product, feeling comfortable with his position in the drug game, Davis replied that he did not need permission to sell where he wanted and that Jones did not own everything. Napier reported back to Jones the incident that had taken place and added the statement that Davis had also said "Fuck the Guy," meaning Jones.

This provided Napier with the ammunition he needed to remove Davis with the permission of his boss whom he was totally devoted to. The next day Napier armed himself accompanied by Maurice "Moheart" Gibbs a cousin of Jones shot Davis dead as he arrived with a team of workers. The rash of shootings and raids started Butch Jones to thinking. His thoughts centered on getting out of the game before it was too late. He had already served time for murder and many of his closest friends and associates were dead or serving long prison sentences.

The Streets Don't Love You Back

By his own accord Jones admitted to having $5 million in cash saved. As the law closed in and attempted to administer a death blow to his organization, Butch Jones fled Detroit along with his wife and their two children in favor of the warm sun and dry climate of Tucson, Arizona.

While authorities conducted extensive searches of several upstate Michigan towns, New York hideouts and Florida hotspots, Butch and family laid low in their new home situated on 3 acres of land. Seal Murray and more than 30 other members of Y.B.I., were picked up and charged with operating a criminal enterprise.

After 3 months on the run, Butch Jones stopped running. With things going from bad to worse, Butch secured his release through the efforts of Otis Culpepper a prominent criminal defense attorney with solid connections in the court system. With a $10,000 price on his head Milton David Jones appeared before U.S. District Judge Ralph Guy Jr., on Tuesday March 22, 1983. Wearing the blue and gray colors which had become the theme of Young Boys attire, Jones was ordered held on a 10 million dollar cash bond.

After refusing to implicate any of the other members of the ring, Jones received a pre-arranged 12 year sentence for running a continuing criminal enterprise.

While serving time, Butch continued to operate Young Boys Inc., through his wife and several others. During this time Butch proved that Young Boys was far from dead when several members of his self-appointed wrecking crew shot and killed 26 year old Rickey Gracey after he led a team of burglars into the Jones house looking for money and dope.

Due to conflicting accounts of what transpired, it is impossible to determine who fired the fatal shots but what is known is that Gracey when found had suffered more than two dozen gunshot wounds. Jones fled Detroit and took refuge in Texas with her then 10 year old son and 6 year old daughter.

The Streets Don't Love You Back

In all Portia and Butch Jones along with wrecking crew members Charles Obey and Spencer Holloway were tried for the killing. Butch had the slaying charge dropped against him in July of 1992 paving the way for him to escape prison for the first time in nearly 9 years. Jones returned to the streets of Detroit which had seen several copycat organizations follow in the mold of the monster he had created years earlier.

The Streets Don't Love You Back

CAREY VINCENT GOINS
Y.B.I Member
1982

On Sunday March 28, 1982 a confrontation between a group of teenagers and two undercover police officers would bring to light one of the most successful and highly organized black gangs this nation has ever produced. At 11:05 officers William Green and Eric Byers were shot after a brief exchange with a 17 year old member of the Young Boys Inc., heroin ring. According to Goins own statement he shot both officers because he feared they were robbers attempting to rob what was then a Y.B.I. stronghold in front of the Ambassador Convalescent Center on Woodward Avenue. Goins happened upon the officers who were questioning a large group of teenagers about violating the cities curfew. Goins reportedly opened fire on the two officers after being ordered to join the group from across the street. After approaching the two officers, Goins drew a handgun from his waist and shot both officers at close range before fleeing into the darkness. Officer

The Streets Don't Love You Back

William Green was pronounced dead at Detroit Receiving Hospital after being struck once in the head while his partner was wounded in the shoulder during the attack. Less than an hour after the shooting, officers arrested Goins near the scene.

Goins involvement with the Young Boys ring was well known to law enforcement officials who used his actions to launch an attack which eventually led to the dismantling of the ring. Goins had a rap sheet which included an entry for possession of a firearm as a 13 year old. A year later Goins was found guilty of attempted robbery and sentenced to probation. His probationary sentence ended in September of 1981 just six months before the deadly encounter. After a swift trial, Carey Vincent Goins was sentenced in recorders court to 12 years to life for murder on November 11, 1982. Little more than a month later officer launched a sweep which netted many of the ranking figures in the notorious drug ring and netted nearly a half million in sales per month.

The Streets Don't Love You Back

Spencer Holloway Portia Jones   Charles Obey

Butch bought his Attorney W. Otis Culpepper
A 1976 Rolls Royce Silver Shadow

The Streets Don't Love You Back

EDWARD HANSERD
DRUG LORD
1986-1991

During the 5 years that Edward Hanserd operated within Detroit's notorious drug world, he was ranked high among the inner city traffickers. The 5'6" Hanserd was known as Big Ed, a name he once claimed to have gotten from the mother of his arch enemy Richard "Maserati Rick," Carter. Edward Hanserd was born and raised in Detroit's urban area attending Osborn High for a time before dropping out and concentrating on a life of crime. During his early years, Hanserd was a small time marijuana dealer receiving most of his product from childhood associates Richard Carter and Demetrius Holloway. Carter and Holloway would go on to become legendary figures dominating the crack craze which struck Detroit during the late 80's. Big Ed Hanserd seeing the success of his childhood associates began making plans to cut himself in for a piece of the pie.

The Streets Don't Love You Back

By the mid 80's Ed Hanserd began making a name for himself by selling marijuana while running the Unisex Salon near Chrysler's Jefferson Avenue plant. The small scale operation provided Hanserd with enough capital to purchase two houses in the 13400 block of Sparling Street which he used to finance the expansion of his own venture into the lucrative crack trade.

Shortly thereafter Hanserd broke ranks with the powerful ring run by Carter and Holloway and became their prime competition. Big Ed and Maserati Rick Carter one of the founders of the drug organization known as best friends became embroiled in a bitter battle of which the cause is not known for certain. Sources close to both men ascertain that the dispute arose from Hanserd's expansion beyond the east side of Detroit into other communities and areas known to have been under the control of best friends while others claim that the problem arose from a debt owed to Carter by Hanserd, whatever the cause of the initial dispute, it provided the spark which lit one of the most violent battles in Detroit's drug world during the 80's.

Hanserd was known to be something of a hot head whose affinity for guns and violence made him a dangerous foe for Carter who used his vast fortune to assemble a squad of killers which would gain notoriety as one of the most efficient killing machines ever to assemble on the east side. Headed by Rockin Reggie Brown, the gang under the name of best friends is believed responsible for hundreds of murders in the inner city area of Detroit during the late 80's into the early 90's. Despite the seemingly long odds of fighting Carter, Holloway and the rest of best friends, Hanserd's business flourished to the point where by 1987 he was deemed a major trafficker after LAPD officers spotted him and several associates tooling around the Sunset strip in a Mercedes 500SE and a brand new Porsche.

When the officers moved in to investigate the young men, they found Hanserd in possession of several sets of

The Streets Don't Love You Back

identification and another new Ferrari in his apartments parking garage. No charges were brought fourth but the episode marked the arrival of Big Ed Hanserd as a mover and shaker on a national scale. Following his return to Detroit, Hanserd sold Unisex Salon to one of his employees in an effort to hide his holdings in the business. Six months later, Hanserd was attacked by Maserati Rick and an associate with automatic weapons.

Though wounded in the stomach during the attack which left him battered, bruised and stitched for months, Hanserd refused to identify Carter as one of his attackers instead choosing to take care of the matter himself. Following the attack, Hanserds longtime girlfriend Stephanie Jacobs purchased a home in Yazoo City Mississippi on Woodlea Avenue. Hanserd soon followed arriving with an entourage of hoods driving Jeeps, a Corvette, Maserati and several Vans. Ed explained the source of his income as coming from his hair salons back in Detroit. Many of his neighbors found this claim hard to believe considering the armed men who surrounded his home and jumped to fill his slightest request. Many of the men would stay in the home when Hanserd would disappear for weeks at a time on business trips. Edward Hanserd managed to avoid getting into big trouble in Yazoo City picking up only a few drunk driving arrests.

Hanserd maintained that he was only coming down to Yazoo in an effort to relax. In spite of his notoriety on a national level, Hanserd spent almost two years building his organization to the point where he was finally able to compete with Carter and best friends but he would soon find trouble and often. In February of 1988, Louisiana state police stopped Hanserd driving a GM van and confiscated a gym bag containing 1 pair of jeans and $198,000 in cash. Ed protested "to no avail," the seizure of the cash stating that the money came from the sale of his hair salon.

The Streets Don't Love You Back

The following month, a Hanserd associate by the name of Nathaniel Wilson was threatened after he was arrested with 31 kilos of Hanserd's product. Three more arrests would follow, all weapon related charges during the summer of 1988. During one of the arrests Big Ed issued the threat of "I am going to get Maserati Rick, and then I am going to get you," to Officer Rico Hardy. In another arrest he was overheard stating to Officer Randy Homan, "Do you know who I am? I am the number one hit man and dope man in the city." In spite of the threats and boasts, law enforcement officials were forced to watch as Hanserd raised bail and walked free after each arrest. Hanserd's final entry into the police ledger during the summer of 1988 came when he was stopped in September driving his convertible red Maserati. During this stop more than $3,000 in cash and a beeper were confiscated. Days later, Hanserd made his move against Carter attacking the 29 year old drug lord outside of a car wash owned by Carter at West 7 Mile Road and Mansfield in the northwestern portion of the city.

In a gun battle which left Carter hospitalized with a wound in his stomach and Hanserd wounded in the arm, neither man was arrested as each declined to identify the other as the aggressor in the incident. Two days later a man entered room 307 at Mt. Carmel Mercy Hospital and pumped several shots into the head and face of the East side crack king. Carter was pronounced dead at 6:01 p.m. Just hours after his death, Carter was announced as a pivotal witness in a drug case. Hanserd was provided an alibi which protected him from the suspicion that he was responsible for the brazen murder when it was learned he had been picked up at the hospital for possession of a firearm resulting from the shooting which had originally hospitalized his deceased enemy.

When questioned about Carter's murder Big Ed denied any knowledge of Maserati Rick's killing but did admit to once throwing a brick through the window of one of Carter's car washes. Hanserd drew unwarranted attention following the

The Streets Don't Love You Back

November 12 disappearance of Carter's best friend and drug partner Demetrious Holloway from a Hamburger stand. The disappearance of Holloway turned out to be a staged event aimed at throwing investigators and enemies like Hanserd off for a time. Once again detained as a possible witness to the fake abduction, Hanserd answered "He's just gone," and "I heard he's just in hiding." Hanserd continued his quest to control the cities crack trade and appeared to have achieved his goal when a man later identified as Lodrick Parker approached 32 year old Demetrius Holloway from behind as he shopped for a pair of socks in the Broadway store at 4 P.M on October 8, 1990. Parker the prime suspect in the murder of

Hallway's partner Maserati Rick had established himself as Hanserd's most intimidating enforcer.

Witnesses reported seeing Parker and another man enter the parking area before calmly entering the store where Holloway was shot. This murder cleared the way for Hanserd to saturate Detroit with his brand of crack known as Tutti-Frutti, which he secured from major California crack dealers such as the notorious Freeway Ricky Ross. Hanserd was conveniently tucked away in jail on gun charges at time of Holloway's murder. Hanserd had continued his unlucky streak of run inn's with law enforcement resulting in the confiscation of a 52 lb. bundle of cash locked in a blue Samsonite suite case which Hanserd claimed contained his underwear. Officers who had stopped Big Ed in January of 1990 driving a two day old Bronco; later found that the cash totaled $369,000 separated into $5,000 increments.

Hanserd did not protest the seizure of the cash as the proceeds of illicit activity. One month after the seizure of the almost half million dollars Hanserd settled his gun charges accepting a probationary sentence and a fine. Several weeks later, Hanserd was arrested once more after Detroit police officers chased Big Ed's white BMW after a home near Outer

The Streets Don't Love You Back

Drive and Gunston was ventilated with automatic weapon fire. The pursuit went through the streets of the east side and ended when the BMW crashed into 3 cars.

Upon reaching the accident scene, officer's found a semi-conscious Hanserd laying just outside the open driver's door and inside the vehicle they found an Israeli made assault rifle and a MAC-10. Investigators later determined that the shots were fired from Hanserd's assault rifle. This was quickly followed by yet another arrest after officer's witnessed Hanserd threaten a man with "I will put a hundred holes in your ass." A search of Hanserd's car which was parked near the incident which occurred on the corner if Linwood and Richton turned up a Korean made 5.56 mm semiautomatic assault rifle fitted with a 30 round clip.

During his life of crime Hanserd had been wounded no fewer than 9 times in three separate shootings. In spite of the frequent arrests, seizures and shootings, Big Ed still managed to turn his dream of running a big time operation into a reality. Investigator's figure that Hanserd's operation at its peak transported an average of 250 keys of cocaine and another 20 keys of heroin from his suppliers in Los Angeles to the territory he carved out on the east side and down into Mississippi where he took refuge from the battle's which raged in Detroit. "Note: a key is street slang for a kilogram of the drug mentioned which weighs 2.2 lbs." The net worth of the Hanserd organization was placed at a conservative $54,000,000 dollars annually. This allowed the then 25 year old high school drop out to drive around in a fleet of exotic cars, live in plush upscale housing while sending jewelry and $200,000 cash to his elderly grandmother in Mississippi. Hanserd was ultimately taken down when Anthony Medina one of Hanserd's California contact's turned and began providing info against big Ed while attempting to keep his end of the operation going. What was sure to be another bloody chapter in the story of Ed Hanserd was averted

The Streets Don't Love You Back

when he received a 3 1/2 to 5 year term for his last gun arrests. Hanserd was put away for good when on May 9, 1991 he was sentenced to serve a 40 year sentence for drug trafficking and federal gun charges. At the time of his sentencing the 28 year old Hanserd lived up to expectations going on one of his famous tirades in which he attacked everyone from the witnesses against him to the judge to the D.A and his own attorney.

The Streets Don't Love You Back

DEMETRIUS HOLLOWAY
DETROIT DRUG LORD
1970s-1990

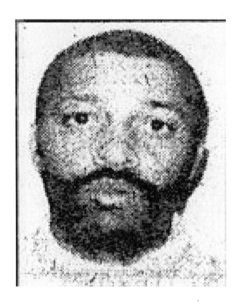

Demetrius was one of the founding members of the infamous Best Friends drug organization, which ruled urban Detroit's multimillion dollar crack trade from the mid to late 80's. Holloway grew up with legendary Detroit figures such as the late Richard "Maserati Rick" Carter also a founding member of Best Friends, and boxing legend Thomas "The Hitman" Hearns.

After working briefly as a postal clerk, Holloway was convicted and sentenced to federal prison after being convicted of burglary in 1980. Holloway's initial prison stay was lengthened after picking up a second conviction for drug trafficking. Upon his release in 1985, Demetrius managed the Chalk & Cue pool hall on West 7 mile Road for William Van

The Streets Don't Love You Back

Lewis. It was from Lewis that Holloway learned the ins and outs of legitimacy and used the pool hall as a front for his drug business. By 1986 Holloway and Carter were running a multi-million dollar drug operation which allowed Demetrius to open 3 sporting goods stores, in addition to purchasing several acres of land in Alabama while setting up Renters Paradise to oversee several Detroit Apartment buildings which allowed him to claim a legal $17,000 in monthly income.

Holloway also claimed to be a professional gambler a habit or business which he claimed to the tune of $288,000 to $780,000 on federal tax returns filed in the late 80's. Holloway was known to make frequent trips to Las Vegas and Atlantic City New Jersey where he once returned with winnings totaling $125,000 after a weekend jaunt. As the 90's came to a close the high profile living and constant battles with drug rivals and authorities led Holloway to stage his own disappearance from and East Detroit hamburger stand. At the time of his disappearance Holloway was fighting the seizure of two of his sporting goods stores, a Mercedes Benz and more than $90,000 in cash. Part of which was taken in 1986 when he was arrested for disorderly conduct. At the time of his arrest, Holloway was carrying $35,000 in cash and lost another $92,000 when federal authorities arrested him outside of a known crack house. Further heat was brought down on Best Friends when customs officers began arresting women bound for Detroit from the Bahamas with kilo packages of cocaine. According to federal documents these women had been paid upwards of $2,000 dollars per trip. In court documents, Holloway admitted to being associated with or knowing members of other Detroit drug gangs including the Curry and Chambers brothers, White Boy Rick Wershe, Frank Usher, Seal Murray and of course Maserati Rick Carter. Beyond these damaging admissions, Demetrius invoked his 5th amendment rights in answering questions about his finances and drug ties. Holloway was dealt a stunning blow when his lifelong friend and partner Maserati Rick Carter was shot and killed as he recuperated from another shooting in September of 1988 in a Detroit hospital.

Following Carter's death, the first person the Carter family contacted was Demetrius Holloway who soon thereafter arranged his own abduction. Absent for several months from the strife and conflict which had claimed his pal, Holloway travelled to Las Vegas where he married his girlfriend Wanda Jean Hardaway the sister of Charles "Chucky" Hardaway, another reputed drug figure. Thirty two year old Demetrius Holloway was gunned down at 4 P.M. Monday October 8, 1990 in a shooting almost as brazen as the one that claimed Maserati Rick more than two years prior. Holloway was shot as he picked out a new pair of socks in the Broadway Department store. Demetrius, who was killed by two shots to the back of the head, had a pistol in his possession as well as $17,000 in cash but did not have the chance to defend himself. Holloway's murder was believed to have been ordered by Big Ed Hanserd another Eastside drug dealer who was known to have been a rival of Holloway and Carter.

The Streets Don't Love You Back

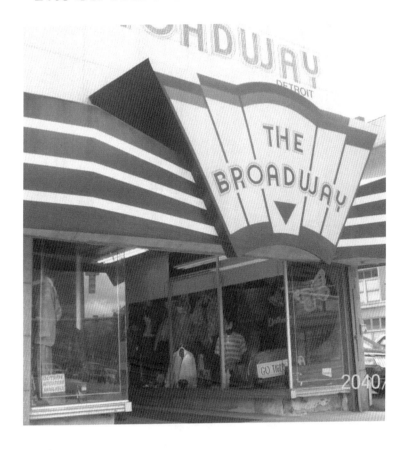

Demetrius Holloway was shot and killed in the Broadway Department store.

The Streets Don't Love You Back

THE CHAMBERS BROTHERS
Chambers Family Drug Ring
1983-1989

Billy Jo Chambers/Larry Chambers

Otis Chambers/Willie Chambers

The Streets Don't Love You Back

The Chambers Organization consisted primarily of 4 brothers from the impoverished town of Mariana Arkansas. The Chambers family lived in the poorest and most backward part of Arkansas. Two of the brothers Billy Joe and Larry by the mid-1980's identified, created and exploited the crack cocaine wave by building two inter-related, well-organized crack distributing organizations that operated on different principles. In 1979, teenage Billy Jo moved to Detroit to continue going to high school. He was living with another family from Arkansas, the Colbert's. Billy Jo became famous for his generosity.

All over the east side, it seemed everyone knew "BJ" the charismatic, bighearted young dealer. Billy attracted a crowd of followers and by the summer of 1984 Billy Joe had expanded his house-based marijuana business into the crack business. The cocaine was selling as fast as he could buy and process it. Willie Chambers, an older brother was a mail carrier. He saved enough to buy some property in the depressed lower east side of Detroit and opened a party store in January 1983. Billy Joe went to work for Willie, running the party store business practically around the clock, where he also sold marijuana. The marijuana business boomed. But after a police raid, Billy Joe moved his business to some cheap houses that he purchased in the "economic and social wasteland" in Detroit. Larry Chambers, born in 1950, was a heartlessly vicious career criminal. He had repeatedly escaped from prison by the time he arrived in Detroit. To discipline his branch of the organization, he either beat or killed employees who broke his rules. For example, one employee was selling plaster chips instead of $8 "rocks" in violation of the rules. Larry and two enforcers beat the man with a wooden two-by-four, a lamp, and a television set, and then dragged the man to the kitchen and poured hot grease on him. Larry's enforcers were called the "Wrecking Crew."

The Streets Don't Love You Back

In 3 short years the gang hit its stride when yet another Chambers brother moved to Detroit after a 5 year stretch in Leavenworth. Larry Chambers provided the experience, focus, direction and capitol needed for the gang to move into the crack cocaine market. In short order Willie and Otis Chambers joined the fray as the groups operation expanded netting them an estimated profit of $42,000,000 easily qualifying them as the richest men to emerge from Mariana.

The Chambers gang would collapse under the weight of justice in 1989 when all of the brothers involved in the operation would be convicted and sentenced to long prison terms. Four brothers from Arkansas, the sons of sharecroppers, grew up to become some of the most notorious drug lords in America. In the 80's Billy Joe, Willie, Larry and Otis Chambers were running a crack enterprise that netted them more than $50 million a year in Detroit. Although crack houses were popular, the brothers considered them to be an organizational nightmare and created "Marlowe's One Stop" in a dilapidated apartment building. They were flying high until Larry's ego got the best of him and he began videotaping drug deals. His home movies were found during a raid of his home and the brothers were convicted in 1988. The indictments of the Chambers gang were accompanied by great hype. The Chambers operated some two hundred crack houses, supplied another 500 crack houses, employed 500 workers, and grossed up to three million dollars a day, according to the federal authorities. The Chambers were all jailed by 1988.

The Streets Don't Love You Back

PONY DOWN
LEROY BUTTRON WILLIS-GUNN

Modeled after the highly successful Young Boys Inc., operation, Pony Down was the brain trust of the Buttrom Willis brothers. Leroy Buttrom the leader of the group followed Young Boys tactics of using juveniles to peddle their product in an effort to confound law enforcement groups who were virtually powerless to stop the legion of preteen dope dealers running drugs for these two groups. Pony Down sprung up from an area near West Seven Mile Rd and Murray Hill in northwest Detroit. Buttrom Willis began focusing in on more profitable locations held true by Sellers employed by Young Boys Inc.

Pony Down infractions upon Young Boys turf resulted in several shootings among the enforcement arms of both gangs. Pony Down was unexpectedly assisted in their expansion efforts when Young Boys leaders were arrested and convicted of drug smuggling, money laundering and tax evasion in 1983. Leroy mobilized and unleashed his troops on areas previously considered out of bounds for his workers. Willis's expansion plans not only included the Young Boys territory but also the recruitment of the best and brightest of Young Boys enforcers, runners and salesmen. Many of targeted chose initially to remain loyal to Young Boys Inc., but Willis and his troops began making them offers they could refuse only under the pain of death. This operation set forth in early 1982 allowed Pony Down to move into the vacuum created with the convictions of Y.B.I. leaders Seal Murray, Raymond Peoples and Butch Jones followed soon thereafter by the fall of Reginald Davis head of the DFG (Davis Family Gang). Within three years of its inception, the Pony Down Crew had reached its goal of replacing the troubled Young Boys Inc., ring as the most lucrative of Detroit's crack gangs. Buttrom and his ring were selling an estimated $100,000,000 a year in sales at their peak commanding an army of approximately 300 soldiers and associates. The former high school dropout and juvenile delinquent impressed all with his great organization and shrew business manner. By 1983 Pony Down had secured former Young Boys stronghold housing project areas like Herman Gardens and Brewster Douglas under the Pony Down flag. Their territory was marked by the presence of graffiti proclaiming "I Pony Down". Members of the Pony Down crew were identifiable by the Pony brand of shoe that they wore. Buttrom Willis was aided in running his empire by his brothers Walter and Anthony, Robert Latinee and Willie Birch Dawson. Pony Down was brought down by federal efforts in 1985 after several high profile shootouts with members of a resurgent Young Boys Inc., crew. Willis and his entire leadership squad were arrested and ultimately sentenced to prison terms. Willis himself received a six and a half year sentence for directing the murderous ring.

The Streets Don't Love You Back

MURDER ROW
HAROLD MORTON

Specializing in the importation of heroin, Harold Morton came to dominate Detroit's urban drug trade during the 70's. Morton was a key contributor in the heroin fraternity which included such notables as New York's Frank Matthews, Leroy "Nicky" Barnes and Ish Muhammed and Frank James, Chicago's Willie "the wimp," D.C.'s., Mace Brown, Earl Anthony Garner, Warren Christopher Robinson and Linwood Gray, Philadelphia's Black Mafia godfather and L.A.'s., Thomas "Tootie" Reese. Morton employed a crack team of gunmen to enforce his will and collect debts chief among them Frank "Nitti" Usher and Chester Campbell Wheeler. Morton's reign ended shortly after he was arrested along with Hilda Singleton aka Hilda Hughes and charged with conspiracy in the 1977 murder of 24 year old Sandra Jones. Morton paid Michigan taxi driver Thornell McKnight the paltry sum of $3,500 to kill Jones after she had agreed to testify against

The Streets Don't Love You Back

Morton in an international smuggling trial. Jones had been arrested along with Morton as the pair retrieved her baggage containing a load of European heroin at Kennedy Airport in New York. The November 18, 1977 arrest broke the back of Morton's organization and set in motion a series of events which led to Morton's downfall. An investigation into the activities of L.A.'s Tootie Reese snagged Morton and several of his associates. After having been found guilty in Jones murder Morton was sentenced to life in federal prison where he continues to serve his time at the Federal facility in Milan Michigan.

The Streets Don't Love You Back

DEAN PARKER AND TANK BLACK

The unlikely alliance of William "Tank" Black a successful sports agent and Dean Charles Parker, a former second rate basketball player turned drug dealer was brought to light in a case which received tremendous media attention. Tank Black counted among his clients Detroit Lions wide out Jermaine Crowell, Jacksonville Jaguars running back Fred Taylor and a host of others. Dean Parker at 6'7" 205 lbs. was a former aspiring basketball star who turned his attention to illicit activity when it became clear that he held little chance of a professional career in hoops. Authorities found that Parkers drug ring smuggled 1,000 kilos of cocaine a month in the Detroit area. Parker turned to Black to help him set up and ship money to an offshore bank account in the Caribbean. Parker disappeared along with his wife and two children in June of 1998 when authorities began closing in on him. With Blacks help, Parker was believed to have fled the country yet remained on the run until finally succumbing in a vicious gun battle with federal agents. Tank Black's fate was decided in a court of law. It was found that Black continued to conduct

The Streets Don't Love You Back

shady business deals bilking one South Carolina investor while stealing money from his sports clientele. Tank Black was sentenced to nearly 7 years in prison for his role in money laundering, fraud and drug smuggling.

The Streets Don't Love You Back

KALASHO/AKRAWI SYNDICATE
KAIRI KALASHO
DRUG LORD
1986-1989

The Motor city has seen its fair share of violent and financially successful drug rings, few if any came close to matching the accomplishments of the Chaldean syndicate headed by young Khairi Kalasho. Groups such as Young Boys Inc., Best Friends, the Curry and Chambers brothers all earned millions from their sale of illicit drugs like crack and heroin, but all were dependent upon someone else to supply them with the bulk of their inventory. Only the operation headed by Reginald Davis operated on the level of the Kalasho syndicate. At the height of their success, the Kalasho's moved an estimated 100 kilos per month secured from agents of the Medellin Cartel. One of two prominent connections the group made to ensure a steady supply of product for their customers

The Streets Don't Love You Back

in and around the Detroit area. While investigators place the number of Kalasho henchmen at a high of 200, the nucleus of the group was comprised of syndicate namesake Harry Kalasho, his cousin Ray Akrawi, Basil Mezy and Ead Ballo. Kalasho organized a group of close friends and relatives transforming them from a collection of small time peddlers into a multi-million dollar international crime syndicate in little more than two years. Kalasho's charm, quick wit and easy smile endeared him to his most trusted henchmen, but he enforced his rule with ruthlessness unmatched by his foes.

The Kalasho organization suffered a series of debilitating setbacks highlighted by the seizure of 100 kilos of cocaine in route from Florida and the shooting of Khairi "Harry" Kalasho a year later. Kalasho died of his wounds on February 20, 1989 making way for the ascent of his 21 year old cousin Ray Akrawi to succeed him as the head of the syndicate. Akrawi's reign would be marred by his attempts to avenge his cousin's death ultimately costing him a year and a half in prison. Ray's father Louis made a halfhearted attempt to continue the operation but was quickly caught and sentenced to a long prison term for murder.

This closed the books on the Kalasho/Akrawi crime syndicate as a major player in the drug market. The family name would become front page news later when a former employee of the family owned Prestige Barbecue gunned down four members of the family in a robbery. Khairi Kalasho was the youngest of four Iraqi born brothers who arrived in the US before young Harry was old enough to enroll in school. Settling among the small but close knit Chaldean community, The Kalasho clan learned the hardships that life in this country could bring when Harry's father Sakir was killed in a car crash in 1974. Young Harry was taken in by his uncle Louis

The Streets Don't Love You Back

Akrawi a previous autoworker that had opened his own restaurant and party store. While Akrawi held the appearance of a respectable businessman on the surface, the residents of the Chaldean community recognized him as their version of the local mafia boss. During the hours that young Harry spent following his uncle around he witnessed some of the acts that made his uncle a local legend. Among these acts were the time in a fit of rage Akrawi put a whole in a tavern wall with a powerful head butt. In time, Harry became his uncle's right hand man running errands for the older more experienced gangster. In spite of the close bond shared between uncle and nephew, there was a marked difference in the two.

Where Akrawi was loud and rough, his nephew was quiet and reserved. While Akrawi's looks were hardened by his frequent brawls, Harry was considered roughly handsome with blond hair and large eyes which made him look several years younger than he really was.

While gaining invaluable experience dealing with his uncle Louis, Harry was also exposed to a rougher side by his brother Bahaa described by the local police as the leader of a strong-arm gang of thugs. Bahaa would be shipped off to prison in 1984 after he and his gang of flunkies murdered an elderly woman during a home invasion robbery. Sentenced to life without parole, the Akrawi family insists the case was a frame up. Another brother Dhia introduced Harry to drug dealing an activity which led to an 8 1/2 to 20 year jail term being dropped in his lap in 1985. Following the conviction of two of his brothers, Harry began dealing small quantities of cocaine and weed. Within two years with the help of his cousin Ray Akrawi, young Harry was dealing cocaine in mass quantities and had secured a steady supply from a contact with direct ties to the Medellin cartel. With one phone call, Harry Kalasho replaced Best Friends and the Jones Organization as the major players in the Detroit cocaine market. Along the way Harry took on a persona which was much like that of the fictional movie character Scarface who ruthlessly clawed his way to the top.

Ead Ballo one of his top men was instructed to contact Anthony Montello and Joseph Frontiera, two agents of the Medellin cartel operating out of Tampa Florida. Finally, after several failed attempts a deal was then made and the Kalasho organization became the first operation since the dismantled Davis Family Gang to deal with a cartel on a major scale. Within a year's time business was so good that federal investigators learned of the Kalasho desire to launder more than $8,000,000 in cash. This led to a sting which would expose the hierarchy of the group and their method of operation. Federal agents reported several trips involving key members of the Kalasho group to Miami and Tampa looking to increase their allotment of cocaine which varied from 50 to 100 kilos per month. Presiding over an area which included a section of Woodward and 7 Mile Road, Harry bought several new cars including a Mercedes as well as a home for his mother in Bloomfield Township.

Nothing could go wrong it seemed until federal agents seized a shipment of cocaine bound for Detroit in the back of a semi. The loss of the 100 kilo shipment sent members of the Kalasho group scurrying to meet the demands of their customers. In the ensuing investigation, Kalasho lost his Tampa Florida contact in Montello and Frontiera who pled guilty to drug trafficking and two of his top guys in Basil Mezy and Nick Konja who escaped the drug charges by pleading guilty to money laundering. It would take another 3 months to get things up and running again but thanks to the exhausted efforts of Kalasho the motor city connection was receiving an average of 32 kilos per month from south Florida. Harry struck gold in New York when he was able to secure the shipment of 500 kilos of cocaine. With his business booming like never before, Harry began to greedily fear competition from two local dealers one of which was a longtime friend and comrade. In spite of his success in obtaining the 500 kilo shipment, Harry complained to an underling that Sam Gaggo was blocking another contact which would ensure that his organization would never again face the shortage they did with the loss of Montello and Frontiera. To solve this dilemma Harry contracted with two Detroit killers to eliminate his competition for the price of $10,000. At a subsequent meeting Harry relayed that he was anxious to have the killing go down because he had learned that Gaggo had put a contract out on his life upping the price to one kilo for Kalasho's head. According to the testimony of one of the killers Harry took the two on a tour of the area's Gaggo was known to frequent before the two set out to fulfill the contract on November 17, 1988. After spotting Gaggo walking toward his Honda the pair sped up to the unsuspecting dealer and pumped him full of led. Gaggo died cowering behind his cars steering wheel. Never satisfied and increasingly paranoid about rival dealers encroaching on his territory, Harry met with his personnel a month after the Gaggo killing and announced that Munthir Salem a friend who was also dealing cocaine had to die as he was starting to get into Harry's area. Harry detailed that he found out that Saleem was getting his dope from Los Angeles and wanted him out of the way. Pleased with the work of the two men hired to kill Gaggo, Kalasho offered up $10,000 dollars with a bonus clause of an extra $10,000 if the pair would kill Saleem and decapitate him throwing his head in the middle of 7 Mile road as a message to any future competition. Four days later Saleem was gunned down by the same two hit men who passed on the bonus. Emboldened by the success of the first murder, the two hit men were sloppy and did the shooting from their personal vehicles which lead to their arrests. The two fearing life behind bars began telling all they knew to investigators who eagerly jotted down each word.

In spite of sitting atop the most successful drug gang in the city, Harry Kalasho's greed and insecurity led directly to his downfall as the contracted murders of Sam Gaggo and Munthir Saleem were about to drag him down. As the two hired killers sat out of reach telling all they knew about the two Kalasho ordered killings, Raed Jihad emerged as the Saleem family spokesman meeting with police agreeing that in order to get Kalasho they would have to work with one of the killers. Oakland county prosecutor Jeff Butler met on several occasions with Jihad including the night of February 3, 1989. Later that night, Jihad would gun Harry Kalasho down in retribution for the murder of Munthir Saleem. Gravely injured, Kalasho hung on for 17 days before dying as a result of the wounds inflicted by Jihad. In spite of his ruthless desire to be the only source of cocaine in Detroit, Harry Kalasho held a strange appeal recognized by those who worked for him and those who worked to put him away. One federal DEA agent remarked "he had charisma," while yet another law enforcement official remarked "we get hoods in here and they get tears in their eyes talking about him, he had that kind of power and attraction." In a world where ambition and desire can make you king for a while, Harry Kalasho spent two years atop the heap before some things he valued a great deal brought him down; Loyalty, Tradition and Revenge.

The Streets Don't Love You Back

RAGHEED AKA RAY AKRAWI
KALASHO LIEUTENANT
1986-1989

Born in Iraq, Ragheed aka Ray Akrawi was the first cousin and closest companion of Harry Kalasho. In spite of being cousins, the two grew up more like brothers after Ray's father Louis took Harry in following the death of his father in a car crash which severely injured Harry's older brother Tahrir. Louis once an autoworker dabbled in a variety of enterprises at one time or another owning a party store and restaurant. He was also suspected of being a member of a Chaldean crime syndicate which moved small amounts of narcotics and extorted money from the small close knit Chaldean community in the Detroit area. 3 years younger than Harry, Ray took a back seat to Harry when it came to criminal dealings but showed enough intelligence to acquire an exalted position within his cousin's growing criminal syndicate. By the age of 18, Ray Akrawi was in charge of a crew of 20 underlings known as Ray's boys who operated along 7 Mile Road between Woodward and John R. Ray's boys supplied cocaine to mid-level dealers who in turn supplied the numerous crack houses located in Detroit. So successful was Ray in running his operation that he purchased a custom money green Mercedes at a cost of $75,000. Ray became more active in acquiring the rings supplies from various sources following the arrest and conviction of Basil Mezy in June of 1988. Federal agents followed Akrawi as he made several trips to south Florida to secure shipments of cocaine in the 25 to 50 million dollar range. Akrawi renewed the Tampa connection between the Kalasho group, Montello and Frontiera by way of a Columbian national with an import-export business in Miami. While Ray was in on the initial meetings between Kalasho, Montello, Frontiera and Hector Alvarez, he was conspicuously absent during the final days of negotiation between the groups. This connection eventually supplied the Kalasho organization with an estimated 500 kilos a month winding through a pipeline from Miami to New York and eventually finding its way to Detroit. Federal authorities had taken note of Ray's lavish life style which included a fleet of custom cars, jewelry and a 2 week vacation to Greece while claiming to earn a mere $2,400 a year as a grocery clerk. Ray Akrawi's involvement in the Kalasho drug ring took yet another leap when his cousin was shot and killed in February of 1989. Akrawi allegedly stalked his cousins suspected killer before issuing the order which led to the murder of the suspected triggerman Raed Jihad outside of a Detroit coffee house. Ray was tried twice for the murder but never convicted. Authorities were successful however in securing an 18 month jail term for a firearms violation in August of 1990. While serving that term, Akrawi was named in a grand jury indictment which named him, his father and 7 other members of the organization with drug conspiracy. Ray along with Basil

The Streets Don't Love You Back

Mezy, Nick Konja and Basam Jarges among others were eventually convicted on the charges.

The Streets Don't Love You Back

KALASHO BASIL MEZY
LIEUTENANT
1986-1989

As a lieutenant in the Kalasho Organization, Basil Mezy acted as the contact man between the Kalasho suppliers operating out of Tampa, Florida. Mezy along with Ead Ballo and Najah (Nick) Konja were among the highest ranking members of the ring answering directly to Kalasho's cousin Ray Akrawi. Mezy was among a contingent of Kalasho supporters who flew down to Tampa in the spring of 1986 and cemented the agreement which transformed the Kalasho group from a small time outfit dealing in ounce deals to a major league competitor capable of filling multi-kilo orders. The ground breaking deal called for Joseph Frontiera and Anthony Montello to supply the Kalasho ring with a steady stream of Columbian cocaine secured directly from the Medellin cartel. The details of the deal top months to iron out

The Streets Don't Love You Back

but once things got rolling. The Kalasho group became the first major ring since the dismantling of the Davis Family Operation to independently secure their product. Within a year, federal agents watched as Mezy and Basam Jarges delivered $600,000 packed in two suite cases to Jaime Giraldo a Columbian national who along with his brother Norberto distributed cocaine for the Medellin cartel from a base in New York. Over the next four months payments exceeding $8 million were delivered by Mezy to the Giraldo brothers. Basil Mezy's run as a top member of the Kalasho operation ended on June 12, 1988 with the seizure of a semi-trailer at I-75 and West Road. Federal agents found 100 kilos of Kalasho cocaine hidden among a load of bananas. Soon after the seizure, Mezy, Jarges and their contact to the Medellin cartel were arrested. Mezy and Jarges pled guilty to money laundering in exchange for reduced sentences.

The Streets Don't Love You Back

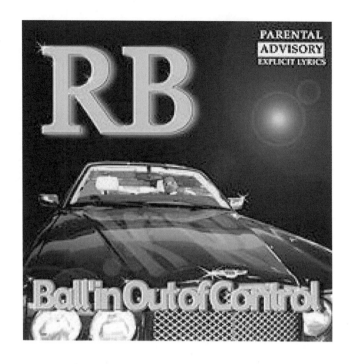

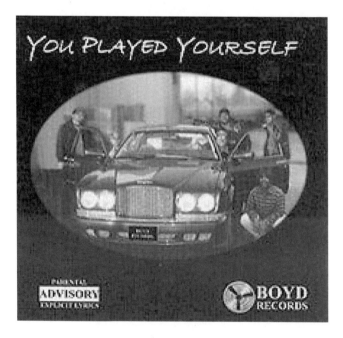

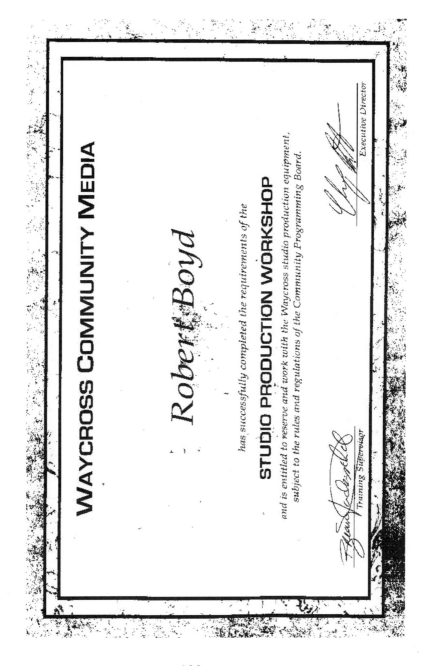

The Streets Don't Love You Back

Mother Vernon Boyd, Robert Boyd and GW

The Streets Don't Love You Back

Robert Boyd with sister Fran

The Streets Don't Love You Back

Sylvester "Sonny" Long, Lieutenant of 430 Crew in 1980"s and Robert Boyd Co-Founder and Boss of 430 Crew in 1980"s

Twista, Slim Goodie and Robert Boyd

The Streets Don't Love You Back

Magic Johnson and Robert Boyd

Group 112 and Robert Boyd

The Streets Don't Love You Back

Robert Boyd and Rapper Slim Goodie

Robert Boyd and R&B Singer Ginuwine

The Streets Don't Love You Back

Rob Boyd and Rapper Jadakiss

The Streets Don't Love You Back

Rob Boyd and R&B Singer Donell Jones

DJ Paul, Rob Boyd, Juicy, Three 6 Mafia

The Streets Don't Love You Back

Rob's friend, Freeway Ricky Ross
Ex Drug Kingpin from Los Angeles. CA.
Released from Prison on May 4, 2009
Welcome Home

The Streets Don't Love You Back

Pretty Cool, Boyd Records first artist in 1995,
Rob Boyd

Rob Boyd and Steve Brown, President of Promotions

The Streets Don't Love You Back

Kyle, Rob and BW
Childhood friends on Galster Street

Lawrence, Marlon, Rob, T. Lemon, and Dave, OG"s from the neighborhood where the Guyton Family lived on Galster Street, and Rob spent his younger years.

The Streets Don't Love You Back

I want to let my sons Michael and Robert know that I love them so much and wherever you go and whatever choices you make in your life I will always support you, love you and be there for you.

Rob with son Robert in 1989

The Streets Don't Love You Back

My son Michael Boyd

The Streets Don't Love You Back

Rob Boyd and Mother Vernon

Mom, Thank you for always praying for me and never turning your back on me, even though, I was always in trouble as a teenager. It's because of you that I made something of my life. I am sorry for all the hurt I caused you in the past. I love you more than life.

The Streets Don't Love You Back

Thank you!

I would like to thank my three brothers Aaron, Lawrence, Dwight and my sister Francetta for always being there for their big brother even when my life was out of control. I love and cherish you I couldn't imagine my life without all of you.
To Elizabeth "Liz," even though we did not know of each other growing up, I am glad you are my sister and proud to be your brother. I love you and look forward to our future and getting to know each other better.

I would like to thank Mike and Janell for being there for me.

Thank you to Mr. Joe Johns and Mrs. Johns for helping me get my TV program "The Keep It Real Show", which I started in 1998.

Thanks and appreciation for Dwight Passmore who helped me run the camera at the "Keep It Real Show". RIP.

Thanks to Tony and Latasha Carson for always being a positive influence in my life.

Thank you to Mr. Dennis Jacobs for taking care of my past websites for many years.
Special thanks and gratitude to my Godparents Tony and Connie Palazzolo for always being a part of my life and guiding me through the storm I love you both.

The Streets Don't Love You Back

I would like to thank Fannie and Earl Richie for being my Godparents and always being there, supporting me and believing in me.

I would like to thank my first cousin Raymond Tarpley Jr. I appreciate all the time you spent revising my book poster and book cover layout.

I would like to thank "LD" Darian for revising and creating the picture on the front cover of my book, for supporting the movement and always being ready to assist me with anything. Much love to you and your wife Hollie.

I would like to give a special shout out to Mr. Steve Agnew at A&A Printing. Thanks for helping me get my message out to the world and Printing my book. Thank you very much for your support and may God bless you and your family.

The Streets Don't Love You Back

Lucinda and Rob Boyd at the Cincinnati, Ohio Public Library where Rob's father, author of sixty four books has an autographed brick on the wall of the second floor.

The Streets Don't Love You Back

Rob Boyd in 1985, Millionaire
Co-Founder of 430 Crew

The Streets Don't Love You Back

Rob Boyd in 2007

The Streets Don't Love You Back

Robert D. Boyd Jr.
Director / Producer / Screenwriter / Singer / Author
Boyd Records
Boyd Publishing
Keep It Real TV Show
Boyd Wear

The Streets Don't Love You Back

THE CINCINNATI ENQUIRER

TEMPO
•the arts•

Sunday April 9, 2000
Mogul in the making concentrates on building musical empire

Going for the record

Robert Boyd has big plans for his record and publishing companies.

BY JIM KNIPPENBERG
The Cincinnati Enquirer

Well, this is a simple enough goal: "I want to be a legend."

Legend, 'eh? Let's see how Robert Boyd is doing:

▶ President of Boyd Records, a 6 year-old Cincinnati and Detroit label with six rap artists, including Mr. Boyd, whose *300 Million Dollar Grind* will be out June 29.

▶ Founder of Slim Goodie Records, a label he set up for Cincinnati actress and rap artist Slim Goodie. Her *Slim Goodie* CD is due any day.

▶ Founder and president of Boyd Films, a Detroit-based company that will shoot a companion film to Mr. Boyd's new CD in June.

▶ Producer and former host of *Keep It Real*, a Warner Cable TV show (11 a.m. Saturdays, repeating five times during the week) full of artist interviews, music gossip, videos and chat.

▶ Founder and publisher of *Keep It Real*, a slick magazine about the urban music industry and its artists. Debuting in July, it will deal with national artists but have Cincinnati and Detroit inserts.

Maybe not a legend exactly, but certainly not bad for a 37-year-old Fairfield and Detroit resident who grew up the oldest of five children in a single-parent household in a tough Detroit neighborhood.

"Coming from the ghetto, I know what it is not to have. And I know what it is to have. Sometimes, I look at myself and think, *me??? This is me???*"

When he feels bad, he remembers "where I came from and what I've done, and then I'm real proud of myself. That I have been able to succeed at something I love.

"You'll see all that when the film's done. It's about a young man from the 'hood, the bad side of Detroit. But he survived all that, the gangs, the violence, the drugs all around him, because he wanted more out of life. And he got it.

"It's *my* story, and something I never could have lived without my mother. She is my strong force and my inspiration." And the reason he wants to be a legend. "I want her to see

Fine, but he still doesn't *look* like a legend. One hand is trying to manage a fat cheeseburger dressed with the works. The other is trying to manage a 3- and 4-year-old (he sometimes steps in when friends have a child-care crisis) with big energy and hands too small for overdressed cheeseburgers.

"I'm working on my short-term goal right now," he says. And that would be? "Financial success. We have been successful artistically, people know us and know they get quality from us. That part was the ground work, now is the final push, to make that pay off.

"I'm looking for things to really start smokin' this summer."

Heaven knows it wasn't smoking last summer, when Mr. Boyd was in the middle of a desperately needed hiatus.

"I took two years off and nurtured myself. Get back on point and figure out what I want in my artists. Some of the early ones had the talent, but had not been, umm, fulfilling expectations. They'd cut a CD, then not want to perform or go on the road."

He realized then that to succeed he needed artists who were talented — and hungry. "As hungry as me ... they had to be driven to succeed.

"That's the kind of team I have now that's making it work. If it keeps going well, I can go into the background. My idea is to put other artists out front — push the ones who can't push themselves."

But as long as he's up front, he'll need to answer some questions.

"Ask me."

The best thing about the Cincinnati music scene ...

Is that we have A. Chiles Promotions and TC Entertainment bringing in quality entertainment here and around the world.

The worst thing about it ...

Is that artists don't stick together on the music scene. They start out here, they make it and they forget Cincinnati. I think that's terrible, because this city could be big. There's a lot of major talent here.

The first thing I'll do after Boyd Records guests but never do ...

I'll continue to shoot higher — for myself and my artists. With gold, the game changes, you have to maintain status and shoot higher all at once. *Slim Goodie* will be the first.

As a small, independent label, one thing I really want to tell the big companies ...

Is to watch out. Boyd Records is right at your doorstep and taking no prisoners.

The biggest obstacle in the way of a small local company ...

Financial, never enough; and sometimes the type of artists you deal with. Distribution is usually the biggest problem, but we have a national distributor, so it's not for us.

One guest I really want to snag on my TV show ...

Russell Simmons, founder of Def Jam Records. I've followed his career since the '80s. He's a true entrepreneur — came from $17 million in the hole to $33 million ahead right now.

One question I always want to ask TV

point in your life? I want to ask, but so many won't let you get that personal. But their answer to that is the story that could save a life — some kid in trouble hears it and, wow, turns around.

One question I wish you'd ask me ...

Not today, but someday, I want you to ask, 'How does it feel to have a platinum album on the wall.'

If I had enough time, I'd like to ...

Be waterskiing, or on a beach chillin', writing more films and songs.

No matter how much time I had, I'd never ...

Cross anyone off or out. Or do anything to lose my credibility. In this business, all you really have is your name — you can live on it forever. Money goes away, but you can always

143

The Streets Don't Love You Back

After spending half his life running the streets and the other half running his own label, Robert Boyd is bringing his televised music showcase home

BY JOE GIULIANI

We're driving through the Warren-Conners projects on Detroit's east side as the sun shines brightly on a Monday afternoon in late March. As we drive along at about 15 mph, a black Detroit police cruiser approaches us going even slower. As it rolls by, the cops in the front seat give us a hard look as we pass. Sonny Long behind the wheel, dark brown skin and gold-rimmed glasses shaded orange under a shiny white ball cap. Robert Boyd in the passenger seat, dressed all in black, brown skin with a black do rag under his ball cap. And me in the backseat, pasty white skin and black-framed glasses.

"They think we're taking you somewhere," says Long.

"To get drugs," says Boyd, finishing the sentence.

We're not getting drugs; we're on a tour of the old neighborhood. This is where Boyd and Long grew up. The hat on Boyd's head reads, "Robert Boyd Records," the record label Boyd started in Cincinnati after he moved there from these projects in 1989.

If this were 20 years ago, Boyd might have been taking me to score drugs.

"I was a kingpin around here," Boyd says. "I started selling drugs when I was 10 years old. I had a million dollars when I was 18."

That was before Boyd realized his life wouldn't last long if he kept doing what he was doing. So in '89 he moved to Cincinnati for a fresh start, a city he had visited a few times and which he felt was a more positive place to live.

After a couple years there, he started Robert Boyd Records. Then, in 1998 he began hosting a music showcase called the *Keep it Real Show*, on cable TV. The show now airs in Cincinnati, San Diego and New York, and beginning the first week of May, it will begin airing here in Detroit on Comcast channel 68. Air times had not been decided as of press time.

The *Keep it Real Show* is taped in San Diego, where Boyd's business and life are now headquartered. The *Keep it Real Show* features national R & B and hip-hop acts with some shows spotlighting local acts from the regions where they air. The format is interviews, live performances and music videos.

Boyd started the *Keep it Real Show* after he appeared as a guest on a locally-aired cable talk show called, "In and Around Cincinnati." The host, Joe John, was impressed with the way Boyd carried himself on camera. He suggested Boyd would do well hosting his own show, and he helped Boyd to put it together and get it started.

"He put a word in for me, and I'll always love him for that," Boyd says.

THE LIFE HE HAD TO LEAVE

Back at the Warren-Conners, Boyd points to a small, brown, brick building in a huge empty field, across the narrow street in front of us.

"That was the pool and the rec center," he says. "Behind was the building I grew up in. They tore those down and built these new ones. It was grimy then.

"And we used to race cars down this street right here, bet $5,000 a pop," he says. "We'd walk from Chandler Park to that street over there, selling drugs all day long."

From pusher

to promoter

This is what Boyd had to leave. The life. The friends, most of whom are either dead or in prison. The attraction of the drug money, which is a lot more real than the power of some piece of paper you might get in some college you've never seen.

But Boyd knew he couldn't stay in Detroit if he wanted to go straight. The connections to the street life were too close at hand.

"Life in the penitentiary or dead, only two ways it could have gone," Boyd says when asked what would have happened had he stayed. "But I was always afraid to let my mom down."

Boyd talks a lot about his mom. He flies in every year for her birthday. And he cancelled our interview two days earlier so he could spend his first day back in town with her. Exactly what a good son would do.

"I talked to my mom one night; I told her I had to get out. She was sad, but she knew that was the best thing for me."

When Boyd started the record label down in Cincinnati, he opened a Detroit office too, to search for talent here. But he shut it down after a short while because those old connections kept trying to get in touch with him through it.

"These guys kept calling me up, saying, Hey why don't you record me, but they were still into bad stuff. A lot of guys on the street think people owe them something, but it starts in you."

For Boyd, the music started in him at a young age.

"All my life I had been singing. My mom used to sing too. Me and my boys would go in the Coney Islands and I'd sing. I'd sing while we were walking up and down the street.

"I really started to take music seriously in 1988, then I moved to Cincinnati the next year."

FROM SLANGIN' TO SINGIN'

We leave the projects and it's on to Strong Avenue, to show me the house Boyd lived in before his mother moved the family to War-ren-Conners. We pass by Burrows Jr. High, one of many schools Boyd attended. We pass the school's football and baseball fields. The grass is thick but all yellow and brown.

"A lot of cats got killed in that field," Boyd says looking dreamily out the car window. "I got kicked out of there at 14. I shot up the school one night."

Across from Burrows is an empty corner lot. Boyd used to live in a house on this lot. Another house that got torched by arsonists and has been torn down. We turn onto Strong and pull up to the curb across from the lot. A guy standing on a front porch starts down the steps.

"That's Robert Boyd," the man calls out.

Boyd gets out of the car, and the two hug. After a brief catch-up of "how you been's?" Boyd leads him back to the car for introductions.

"I always knew he had potential," says Dwayne Weathington. "He was a great singer, I was selling his demos on the corners back then. I'd sell them all, and people would ask for more."

While Boyd is standing on the curb talking to Weathington, Sonny Long tells me about the help Boyd gave him in getting a book published. "He gave me $10,000 to publish and promote my book," he says. "$10,000. And never asked for a penny of it back. I'd do anything for that man."

On the other side of the car, Boyd and Weathington are talking about the old days, and the people they knew. When it is time for us to go, Weathington asks Boyd, "Hey man, can I get a few bucks?"

Boyd turns his back and pulls a small wad of bills from his pocket. He hands a couple bills to Weathington, they say goodbye, and we're off again.

In the car, Boyd says, "I don't know if he'll use it to get high or buy food. But I got to give it."

Boyd moved his operations from Cincinnati to San Diego in order to be in a city with a more thriving music scene. Since then, things have just gone better and better for Boyd. He recently put out a CD of his own music called, "Ballin' Out of Control," and in April he performed in Paris. He even has a line of clothing coming out soon.

And with the success has come an urge to help others. Boyd has a scholarship program set up to help underprivileged kids attend college. Regardless of race, students who have the grades and ambition but lack the money can apply for the scholarship by sending a letter discussing their school and what they hope to do with their life. (see *www.keepitrealshow.com*)

For now, Boyd is looking forward to coming back to Detroit to tape an episode of the show.

"I might open another office in Detroit. We'll see."

144

The Streets Don't Love You Back

LOCAL LIBRARY
EVERYBODYS NEWS MAY 15-21, 1998

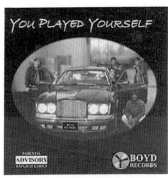

Various Artists You Played Yourself
(Boyd)

If you have yet to experience the world of Cincinnati/Detroit-based Boyd Records, the label's new compilation album, You Played Yourself, serves as a prime introduction.

Released nationally this past May 1, this album should help give these wordsmiths from the heartland the increased exposure they deserve. The untitled opening track introduces you to the crew of R.B., Struggle, Mr. Nastier Nass, Pooh, Tail Picasso, and Rude Boy then takes off for eleven songs of tight rhythms and masterful rhymes. Confidence and attitude exude from each cut, not in a confrontational way, but in a way that makes you smile and say, "Uh huh, that's right." Produced by

Robert D. Boyd Jr. Muzical Mali and Struggle, You Played Yourself works with sparse accompaniments that further highlights the tongue twisting tirades and soulful, R&B-infected interludes. Whether teaming up for a track or just kicking" it solo, the Boyd crew will get your ass (black or lily white) bumpin,, thimpin" and humpin" to the beat.

--Alphonz DeMille

The Streets Don't Love You Back

Cincinnati Post

SONG FOR HOMELESS: Singers LaVern Dukes and P.C. (Pretty Cool) videotaped the song —Make it Happen‖ in Washington Park Tuesday with the help from Southern Ohio College Video Students Erin Giraul and Jeff Winkelman, Boyd Records and P.C., a local musician, pledged half the proceeds from the CD to the Cincinnati Coalition for the Homeless in honor of slain activist Buddy Gray.

146

The Streets Don't Love You Back

THE CINCINNATI ENQUIRER

TEMPO the arts

SUNDAY MARCH 29, 1998

HEARD AROUND TOWN: −Can you believe this? We've gone mainstream. We're running with the big dogs now. That from **Robert Boyd**, President of Boyd Records, a local house specializing in rap. Reasons he's elated? He and his stars-- Struggle, Pooh, RB, Mr. Nastee Nass, and Takill Pikasso are in 60 million households thanks to a weekly TV show, Fast Track to Fame. It's a showcase, shot in North Carolina, to introduce new rap, gospel, R&B, jazz, country and reggae acts. It Aires in 100 cities (locally, it's on at 1 A.M. Sunday on WBQC, Channel 25) with several other cable companies chomping at the bit. Here's more: A local show, **Keep It Real**, is in the works. It's a talk show with videos and live performances by local and visiting acts. Boyd hopes to have it on Warner Cable within a month.

And Boyd's stars are on a national concert tour and gearing up for the May 1 release of −You Played Yourself". The completion CD features several of Boyd Records acts.

The Streets Don't Love You Back

THE CINCINNATI ENQUIRER

TEMPO *the arts*

TUESDAY DECEMBER 9, 1997

Struggle's rap is riding high

Know who needs a round of applause this morning? **Struggle** as well as Cincinnati's **Boyd Records**, a new outfit run by **Robert Boyd**. Rapper Mr. Struggle is riding plenty high with his −You Played Yourself single. So high that **Run D. M. C.** asked him to open a show for them. He did in November at Harpo's in Detroit. That's not all: He has a CD due next summer. But first he and Boyd colleagues will tour: They are in the process of setting up a college campus tour which, Boyd hopes, will take them to every black college in the country. They'll do a Cincinnati date, but it's not firm. Boyd, meanwhile, is in the final stages of a compilation CD named for Struggles single. It will include Pretty Cool, RB, Mr. Nastee Nass and Boyd. Look for it in early 98. But, first one of these: clapclapclap...

The Streets Don't Love You Back

THE CINCINNATI ENQUIRER

TEMPO *the arts*

WEDNESDAY APRIL 9, 1997

BUZZ AROUND TOWN: keeping eyes and ears open. Pssst' has heard.... That there is a new video production house in town and it's already making a mark. That would be Turner-Hader Entertainment, owned by Mark Turner with Matt and Art Hader. Reason we bring it up is because the company made a commotion Tuesday on over-the Rhine's Washington Park. Seems local rap artist P.C. (Pretty Cool is the full name) and a cast of five principals and a three member combo were shooting the video to go with P.C.'s Make it Happen (Boyd Records), a single dedicated to the memory of homeless activist Buddy Gray. The whole troupe--lights, camera, action, and the works--hit the park Tuesday for a shoot that used the neighborhood folk as well as professional actors. The video and P.C.'s *PULL UP* CD should be out in May.

SCENE & HEARD

By Thurgood Ann Williams

October 6, 1997

On the Local Front

The **Leap Skyward** boys, those purveyors of the rock dude aesthetic, have teamed up with their label Alpha Dawg Records to form the Leap Skyward Foundation, an organization aiming to provide some green for local charities, and in doing so joining together all kinds of local bands for a common cause. The first benefit concert takes place this Wed. Oct 15 at Top Cat's where Leap Skyward will join up with an electric mix of tunesmiths including Kid Valance, Mongrel Soup, Thistle and ***Boyd Records*** artists Mont and Struggles. Proceeds from the concert will benefit the Homeless Coalition of Cincinnati. For information on the benefit show call the Leap Skyward hotline, 2420049, or Boyd Records, 230-7084. The leap Skyward Foundation also encourages everyone and anyone to submit requests and ideas for benefits and organizations in need. Write to Leap Skyward, P.O. Box 18162, Cinti., OH 45218.

SCENE & HEARD

By Thurgood Ann Williams

May 15, 1997

Local Releases

This Thursday May 29 marked the release of two new albums on **Boyd Records,** Pretty Cool's Pull Up and Northern Exposure by Mr. Nastee Nass. You can find them in stores or order them through Boyd Records web site at www.boydrec.com. As you might recall, pretty Cool shot a video here in town April 8 for "Make it Happen" a single off the new album written in memory of homeless activist Buddy Gray. With half the profits from the sales of *Pull Up* going to the Cincinnati Coalition for the Homeless. It would indeed be a good thing for you to buy it. For more info on these releases check out the web site or labels Detroit office at 313-340-0422

The Streets Don't Love You Back

SCENE & HEARD

By Thurgood Ann Williams

November 19, 1997

Locals on the Road

Locally based Boyd records is gearing up for the early 98 release of a CD featuring a variety of the label's artists, including Struggle, Mr. Nastee Nass, Pooh and others. And dig this, Struggle will be opening for Run D.M.C. this Wed. Nov. 26 at Detroit. Don't you wish it was you, fuckers? (Boyd Records website: www.boydrec.com)

SCENE & HEARD

By Peter Fontieroy

April 24, 1998

On the Local Front

Boyd Records has teamed up with the *Fast Track to Fame* television show to present some talent on a national level. The national talent showcase airs every Sunday in towns across America and features all types of music including R&B, hip-hop, jazz rock reggae, and more. For more info call Boyd Records at 513-230-7084. Or visit the Boyd website at www.boydrec.com, also set your sights for May 1, 1998 when the Boyd Records compilation CD will hit the stores all over.

(Please Print) NAME _Robert D Boyd_

D.O.B. _____ ADDRESS _P. O. Box 226_

WATER BAPTISM DATE _3/07_ HOLY GHOST BAPTISM DATE _____

PRESENT CHURCH AFFILIATION _GEAT_

SPECIAL REQUESTS AND / OR NEEDS _Prayer_

PHONE ( )

Cinti _Ohio_ _45201_
city   state   zip

REFERRED BY _____

Today _3/07_ You _Robert Boyd_ Have been Baptized in JESUS' NAME at

The Greater Emanuel Apostolic Temple
Cincinnati, Ohio

We are praising God for your decision to pursue the total New Birth/Born Again experience by being obedient to GOD'S WORD according to the Holy Scriptures (Mark 16-18; Luke 24:45-49; Acts 2:38; 8:12; 10:48; 19:5; Romans 6: Col. 2:12 etc.) whereby all your sins have been washed away, forgiven and remitted. However, water baptism is only on part (John 3:5) of your new birth... You must also be born of the Holy Ghost (Holy Spirit) according to the Holy Bible (John 3:5; 7:38-39; ACTS 2:4; 10:44-47; 19-6). The Bible states that as the believers were filled with the Holy Ghost (Born of the Spirit) they spoke in other tongues and magnified God. This Heavenly regeneration experience is awaiting you to completely change your life. If this experience has already happened to you...We say HALLELUJAH!

[ ] Have been filled with the Gift of the Baptism of the Holy Ghost...
Speaking with tongues as the Spirit of God gave you the utterance,
Witnessed by _____ and

Please understand that by being baptized in JESUS' NAME and Spirit filled YOU have NOT joined and/or become a member of the Pentecostal Assemblies of the World, but you have truly joined Jesus and have become a member of the true body of Christ. We will be happy to discuss local church membership if you desire. The remainder of this form is to be completed and signed. Thank you and God Bless You!

(PLEASE PLACE THIS COPY IN YOUR WALLET.)

signature

REFERRALS

OUT OF TOWN REFERRAL

PARTNER'S PHONE NUMBER

YOUR PRAYER PARTNER

Greater Emanuel Apostolic Temple, P. A. of W.
1150 West Galbraith Road, Cincinnati, Ohio 45231
(513) 522-9357 / 522-1150 Pastor Bishop P. A. Bowers D.D.

154

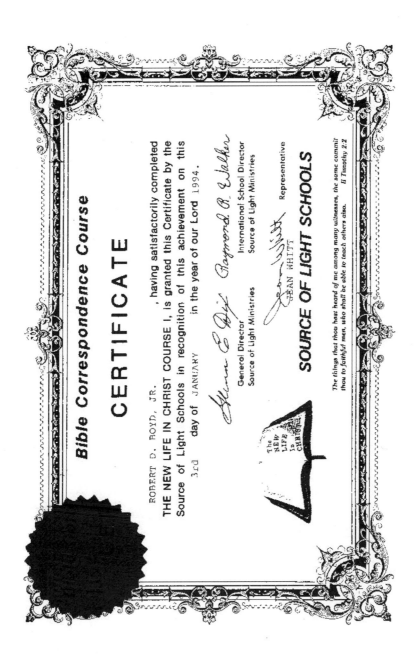

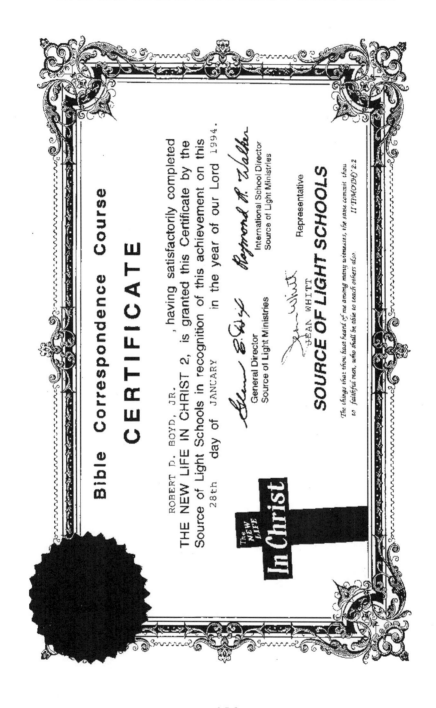

The Streets Don't Love You Back

CLINTON
GORE

November 18, 1996

Mr. Robert D. Boyd, Jr.
Boyd Records
P. O. Box 226
Cincinatti, OH 45201

Dear Robert:

Thank you for writing to me with your concerns about homeless Americans and for sending the cassette to my attention.

Homelessness is a complex problem that is made worse by rising housing prices, a shortage of jobs, crime, drug and alcohol abuse, and mental and physical illnesses. Homelessness can happen to anyone, and it affects everyone.

This crisis requires a wide range of solutions. I have proposed that we increase funding to house homeless citizens and to develop reforms for our health care system so that people who are sick can get the care they need. We must ensure that all Americans have a place to live. We must also provide adequate health care and create more jobs, while fighting crime, reducing substance abuse, and working to end communicable diseases.

Only when we know that all of our citizens have the opportunity to reach their full potential can we say that our society is prepared for the challenges of the future. I commend you for promoting and exemplifying the spirit of caring that is such an integral part of the American character, and I encourage you to act on your ideals.

Sincerely,

Bill Clinton

THE WHITE HOUSE
WASHINGTON

Mr. Robert Boyd
Boyd Records
Post Office Box 226
Cincinnati, Ohio 45201

45201/0226

Thank you so much for your kind gift. I appreciate your
thoughtfulness and generosity. You have my best wishes.

Bill Clinton

The Streets Don't Love You Back

Maternal Grandparents

Mary Guyton
Born August 27, 1921-Died October 5, 1973

William Guyton
Born May 30, 1912-Died June 1, 1981

To my Grandfather your soul can rest now. I have forgiven you for killing my stepfather. Your Grandson is a changed man and I made something of my life even though everyone told my mom that I would be nothing. My soul, my heart and my mind are so free now. I give God the glory for truly touching my life and I can move forward to an awesome future.

The Streets Don't Love You Back

Paternal Grandparents

Julia Ann Boyd
Born April 10, 1912 Asheville, North Carolina
Grandmother was a school teacher for 32 years.
Picture taken in Cincinnati Ohio September 12, 1974

Dr. Robert Henry Boyd
Born May 24, 1902 West Pointe Virginia
Died August 7, 1971 in Pennsylvania
Picture taken on his 65th birthday may 24, 1967

The Streets Don't Love You Back

Martin Luther King III and Rosa Parks
Civil Rights Leaders
Author Robert D. Boyd Sr.
Wayne University
Detroit Michigan
April 4, 1980

The Streets Don't Love You Back

Rosa L. Parks and Author, Robert D. Boyd Sr.

Rosa L. Parks signing autographs after she appeared as a guest speaker at a church in Cincinnati, Ohio on Sep. 28, 1980. Rosa L. Parks was born February 4, 1913 in Tuskegee, Alabama, but was reared in Montgomery. Known as a civil rights pioneer, she spurred the civil rights movement in the late 1950's by refusing to relinquish her bus seat to a white person in December 1955. Rosa Parks wouldn't budge. America did.

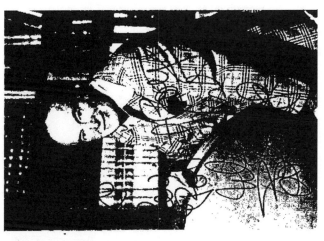

Autograph photo—1980. Comedian Bob Hope.

Note: Photo personally inscribed to me.

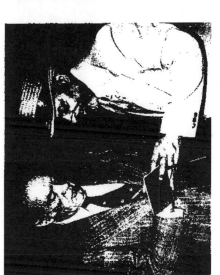

Veteran Comedian—Bob Hope at Age 77. Still has the golden touch to make people smile and laugh.

Whatever it is, if its funny, Bob Hope has been doing it for more then 50 years of show business. Rev. Boyd looks on as the famous comedian autographs and dates his passport book, at the Netherlands Hilton Hotel, in Cincinnati, Ohio, Sunday, November 2, 1980.

Listed: Bob Hope, in the *Guiness Book of World Records* as the most honored entertainer in history, with 44 honorary degrees.

NOTE—Autographed photo—1980 (right) given as a gift, by this author to his hometown library—the Toledo-Lucas-County Public Library—Toledo, Ohio; February 14, 1991.

Federal drug plot case falters

2 defendants dismissed in Chambers brothers trial

By Allan Lengel
News Staff Writer

A drug conspiracy case against the Chambers brothers gang partially unraveled in mid-trial Wednesday when charges were dropped against two of 14 defendants for lack of evidence.

U.S. District Judge Richard F. Suhrheinrich also threatened to dismiss charges against three other defendants if the prosecution did not soon implicate them in the suspected Detroit crack-cocaine network.

Authorities say the Chambers operation once supplied half the city's crack and recruited teen-age workers from Arkansas and Detroit.

Suhrheinrich dismissed defendants Romia Hall of Marianna, Ark., and Alvin Chambers of Flint after the prosecution said government witnesses could not link them to the suspected conspiracy. Alvin Chambers is a first cousin of four Chambers brothers accused of heading the organization.

"Testimony came in different than we had anticipated," U.S. Attorney Roy C. Hayes told the judge. "We cannot meet the burden of proof."

Government witness Morris Killingham on Tuesday was unable to identify Hall as the man who supposedly tried to recruit him into the gang.

A federal indictment charged Hall with recruiting Marianna residents — mostly teen-agers — to work for the Chambers gang in Detroit. Alvin Chambers was charged with conspiracy to distribute cocaine.

Chambers, 32, and Hall, 27, appeared relieved when the judge dismissed them as the trial resumed Wednesday morning.

Hall left the courthouse immediately and could not be reached for comment. Chambers, father of eight children, said he was elated but might sue the government for false charges he believes were based on his last name.

"I didn't have any involvement," he said. "I'm just glad my name is cleared."

Chambers said he had lost his job as a utility assembler for General Motors Corp. in Flint because of the indictment but hoped to be rehired.

He also said the indictment disrupted his family life and embarrassed his children, whose classmates questioned them about the case.

Said William Swor, Chambers' attorney, "I think justice was done. I don't believe he should have ever been indicted."

Jury told of drug gang's terror

By Allan Lengel
News Staff Writer

The Chambers Brothers gang earned up to $200,000 a day selling drugs in Detroit, and kept members in line with such terror tactics as pushing them out windows, U.S. Attorney Roy C. Hayes said Thursday.

Later in the day, former ring member Patricia Middleton told a U.S. District Court jury how two gang members carried a competing pusher's bloodied body from an east-side apartment to a nearby Dumpster.

Attorneys' opening statements and Middleton's appearance marked the first day of testimony in the federal trial of 14 people charged with conspiring to run the Chambers gang drug ring, which investigators say supplied half of Detroit's crack cocaine.

Authorities said the gang recruited teen-agers from Marianna, Ark, and built a booming drug trade with hundreds of employees from 1982-87. The trial before Judge Richard F. Suhrheinrich is expected to last six to eight weeks.

The gang is named after four key members, the Chambers brothers, who grew up in Marianna.

DEFENSE ATTORNEYS used their opening statements to attack the prosecution case, saying it relied too heavily on witnesses with criminal records. Some witnesses have plea bargained to have past charges dropped or reduced, defense attorneys said.

"That is the lowest form of testimony the government can present, someone who is trying to save his skin," said William E. Bufalino II, attorney for defendant Kevin Duplessis.

Defense attorney Bernard Cohen countered Hayes' description of the trial — involving defendants from both Detroit and Marianna — as *A Tale of Two Cities*, a reference to the Charles Dickens novel.

"After the evidence, you will be reading a different book," Cohen said. "It will be *Much Ado About Nothing*."

Middleton, 33, appeared nervous as the first prosecution witness. She was reluctant to glance at the defendants and was at times teary-eyed.

In addition to seeing the pusher's body dropped in a Dumpster, Middleton said she saw Larry Chambers use a chair leg to beat a gang member for selling soap in place of crack.

SHE ALSO testified about the gang's strict rules.

"If you got caught (by police) and open up your mouth, you're dead," Middleton said, referring to one such policy.

She said another gang member was beat-en with a baseball bat and a third was pushed out of a window on the third floor of her apartment building.

"I saw Marlo shove him out the window, the front of the building," she said, not elaborating on what happened to the gang member.

Middleton testified that gang leader Larry "Marlo" Chambers rented several apartments in the building where she lived to use as crack houses.

In July 1986, she said she agreed to collect money for the gang from crack houses around Detroit, but only after Chambers threatened to hurt the man she lived with if she did not cooperate.

Middleton said she made $500 a week until January 1987 when Larry Chambers learned she had spoken to a Detroit narcotics officer. Chambers, she said, put a gun to her head and threatened to kill her if she talked again.

Man shot to death: Two masked
gunmen shot to death a 23-year-old **Detroit**
man and critically wounded a 28-year-old
Detroit woman who sat in a parked car outside a party store on the city's east side Saturday afternoon, police said. The man,
whose identity police would not disclose
pending notification of his family, was pronounced dead on arrival at Detroit Receiving
Hospital shortly after the 2:45 p.m. incident.
He had been shot in the head. The woman
was in critical condition at Detroit Receiving
Hospital with a gunshot wound to the stomach. Police said the two were sitting in a
Mercedes outside the H&J Party Store on
Moran near Gratiot when two men in a second car pulled up and fired.

The Streets Don't Love You Back

On Saturday, Stephen O'Neal Washington, 23, described by police as a Detroit drug dealer, was killed by two masked men firing semiautomatic weapons as he sat in his Mercedes Benz in front of a party store.

Investigators said Washington was killed at 2:40 p.m. as he sat in his car in front of the H & J Party Store, 4174 Moran.

Narcotics officers said Washington was an associate of Richard E. "Maserati Rick" Carter, 29, of Detroit, a reputed drug dealer who was shot and killed Sept. 13 in his hospital bed at Mt. Carmel Mercy Hospital.

Washington was identified in a 1987 murder-torture trial as the operator of a crack house at 2165 Farnsworth. He was not charged with drug trafficking or any other offenses in the slaying.

He was convicted of illegally carrying a concealed weapon in November 1986 and served 13 months in prison.

Police said Sevina Williams, 28, of Detroit, a passenger in Washington's car, was wounded. She is in critical condition at Detroit Receiving Hospital, police said.

Warrant issued in killing

An arrest warrant was issued Wednesday for Lodrick Parker, 29, who is suspected of killing reputed Detroit narcotics dealer Richard E.

(Maserati Rick) Carter on Monday in his bed at Mt. Carmel Mercy Hospital in Detroit.

Police said they have been searching for Parker and a second man who acted as a lookout at the hospital.

Parker

Police described Carter as a top cocaine dealer on Detroit's east side who was involved in a narcotics war.

Family, friends give reputed drug dealer a flashy farewell

By Jean Gadomski
News Staff Writer

Hundreds of mourners showed up Friday for the wake of a reputed cocaine dealer, who was laid out in a casket outfitted with rubber car tires and a chrome Mercedes grill.

At least 20 marked Detroit police cars encircled Peace Chapel on West Seven Mile in Detroit in a discreet but continuous patrol of the gathering.

Richard E. "Maserati Rick" Carter, 29, was shot to death Monday night by a gunman who walked into his room at Mt. Carmel Mercy Hospital.

Carter had been a patient there since he was wounded in a shooting last Saturday.

"THESE ARE all his friends," said Dimitry Holloway, greeting the crowd at the door of the funeral home. Inside, some of the women mourners cried softly.

"He had lots of friends, enough to fill Tiger Stadium.

Police theorize Carter, said to be a major cocaine dealer on the city's east side, was killed by a hit man who came back to finish the job in the hospital.

At Friday's wake, two flower arrangements in the shapes of cars were placed near the casket, apparently decorated in recognition of Carter's nickname "Maserati," an expensive Italian sports car.

He had the name because he has expensive tastes, friends said. So did many of Friday's mourners, who showed up in Rolls Royces, Mercedes and Cadillacs.

One flower arrangement, about two feet by four feet, spelled "Maserati Rick" with red letters against a white-flower background.

An arrest warrant in Carter's slaying has been issued for Lothrick Parker, who was still being sought Friday.

ABOUT 60 of the mourners were standing on the street in front of the funeral home when a Channel 7 television news crew pulled up. The mourners scattered as soon as the television crew turned on its lights and began videotaping the exterior of the funeral home. When the cameraman moved to the parking lot, one of the building mourners stared, began walking in an opposite direction.

One man, who declined to give his name, said he was one of Carter's neighbors, and that Carter had his good points.

"What kind of man was Maserati Rick?"

"Flashy," the man said.

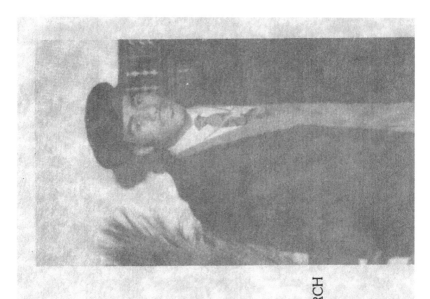

In Remembrance
Of
Our Beloved

Richard Earl Carter

July 31, 1959 — September 12, 1988

Saturday, September 17, 1988 — 2:05 p.m.
CHRIST CORNERSTONE MISSIONARY BAPTIST CHURCH
10905 Mack Avenue At Lemay
Detroit, Michigan 48214
Dr. Obie Mathews, Officiating

The Streets Don't Love You Back

January 24, 1965 - October 10, 2000

*A Celebration of
The Life and Homecoming
For One of Gods Children*

Larry Brent Thompson

Services to be held: Monday, October 16, 2000 Family Hour – 10:00 a.m.
Funeral Services – 11:00 a.m.
Second Ebenezer Baptist Church 2760 E. Grand Blvd. Detroit Michigan

Officiating: Pastor Charles Thomas
Rev: Edgar Vann – Sr. Pastor

The Streets Don't Love You Back

August 27, 1963 – August 4, 2001

A Celebration of
The Life and Homecoming
For one of God's Children

Darryl Jackson Dijon

Services to be Held:
Thursday, August 16, 2001
Family Hour – 11:00 a.m.
Funeral Service – 12:00 p.m.

Swanson's Chapel 806 E. Grand Blvd.
Detroit MI 48207

The Streets Don't Love You Back

May 23, 1962   November 25, 1982

In Remembrance of
Our Beloved

Antonio Cortez Corbin

THURSDAY, DECEMBER 2, 1982
2:00 P.M.

CHAPEL OF
CANTRELL FUNERAL HOME
10400 Mack Avenue
Detroit, Michigan

Rev. V. S. Johnson, Officiating

The Streets Don't Love You Back

May 26, 1955   ~   March 30, 1982

In Remembrance Of Our Beloved

Gary Charles Hunter

Tuesday, April 6, 1982 2:00 P.M.

Swanson Funeral Home Chapel
806 East Grand Boulevard
Detroit Michigan

Chapel Minister, Officiating

The Streets Don't Love You Back

September 4, 1961   June 17, 1983

In Loving Memory

of

Douglas Kenneth Stewart, Jr.

WEDNESDAY, JUNE 22, 1983
1:00 P.M.

CHAPEL OF
CANTRELL FUNERAL HOME
10400 Mack Avenue
Detroit, Michigan

Rev. R. W. McClendon, Officiating

The Streets Don't Love You Back

March 8, 1959   May 14, 1981

In Loving Memory

Of

Raymond Dwight Solomon

Wednesday, May 20, 1981
3:00 p.m.

Swanson Funeral Home Chapel
806 East Grand Boulevard
Detroit, Michigan

Chapel Minister,
Officiating

Warning Signs:
That Your Child May Be Involved with a Gang:

Admits to "hanging out" with kids in gangs. They show an unusual interest in one or two particular colors of clothing or a particular logo. Has an unusual interest in gangster-influenced music, videos, movies, or websites.
Uses unusual hand signals to communicate with friends. They have specific drawings or gang symbols on school books, clothes, walls, or tattoos.
Comes home with unexplained physical injuries (fighting-related bruises, injuries to hand/knuckles), Carries a weapon.
Has unexplained cash or good; such as clothing or jewelry. Getting in trouble with the police. Exhibits negative changes in behavior such as: withdrawing from family, declining school attendance, performance, behavior, staying out late without reason. Displays an unusual desire for secrecy. Exhibits signs of drug use, breaking rules consistently and speaking in gang style slang.

The Streets Don't Love You Back

A List of Books and Literature Published by Robert D. Boyd Sr. in the
Library of Congress, Copyright Office, Washington, D.C.
1965-1997

Youth Today, April 12, 1965©
A Thirsty World, January 10, 1966©
A Hospital Room, September 20, 1966©
Born a Prophet, October 14, 1966©
A Prosperity Prayer, December 25, 1966© 365 Days of God's Love,
February 3, 1967©
Prophecy is Real, February 13, 1967©
A Mighty God, April 10, 1967©
My Mother Prayed, May 14, 1967©
Inspired by God, June 12, 1967©
Books Published by Rev. Robert D. Boyd October 14, 1967©
A Healing Prayer, December 1, 1967©
A Memorial in Honor of Martin Luther King,
Let His Dreams Come, April 26, 1968©
God's Gift to the World-A Little Child, March 1, 1968 ©
Brighter Day Ahead, June 7, 1968©
Determined to be Educated, June 14, 1968©
Picture Post Card bearing pictorial illustration-partial view of
Mrs. Julia
Ann Boyd and son, Rev. Robert D. Boyd,
August 11, 1968©
Picture Post Card bearing pictorial illustration-full view of
Mrs. Julia
Ann Boyd and son, Rev. Robert D. Boyd, August 11, 1968© A
President's prayer, January 17, 1969©
A Religious Greeting Card-Look Where he has Brought You From: A
mighty long ways, January 1, 1969 ©
God's Will, September 24, 1969©
God Speaks to Prophet, December 29, 1969©
Hell on Earth, July 1, 1971©
The Mansion That God Allowed Me to Visit-The Dodge Mansion:
Grosse Pointe, Michigan, August 20, 1973©
Let the Works I've Done, Speak for Me, February 19, 1974©
When She Spoke-Jeane Dixon, Author and Columnist,
December 11, 1994©
World Leaders Hunt Solutions to Nation's Tragic Times,
April, 1975©
A Millionaire in the Spirit, June 17, 1975©
God's Library-The Storehouse of Knowledge, August 7, 1975©
Parents Must Earn the Respect of Children, December 18, 1975©
The Visions of a Thousand Tomorrows- Bicentennial Salute

The Streets Don't Love You Back

1776-1976, September, 2 1976©
As The Lord Reveals It to Me, August 21, 1976©
Gods Way Is the Right Way, February 1, 1977©
A Better Education Means a Better Future, February 3, 1977 ©
Work Your Way Out of Poverty-In Memory of the Greatest Gospel
Voice of Our Time-The Late Mahalia Jackson, February 23, 1977©
The Black Boys Day Has Come-Photo of Rev. Boyd and Movie Actor
Louis Gossett Jr. on Cover, March 24, 1977©
Road Map to Success, December 1977©
If at First You Don't Succeed, Try Again, January 1979©
I'm Feeling the Presence of the Lord-Good Friday,
April 3, 1979©
Be Thankful Today, May 1979©
Collecting Antiques as a Hobby in This Fast Changing Age,
June 1979©
The Passing of an Old Year and the Dawn of a New Day,
January 1981©
Why Aren't You Smiling, August 1981©
1981 Christmas Postcard-Count your Blessings, November 1981©
How Does One Say He's Sorry-Poem, February 5, 1982©
The Key to Heaven's Grocery Store-Poem, October 13, 1982©
The School of Hard knocks, December 28, 1982©
Because I Am Somebody-Poem, March 8, 1983©
I am your Friend-A Friendship Greeting Card, March 21, 1983©
What is Your Ambition in Life as of Today, June 6, 1983©
Historically Speaking-Blacks in America, 1987©
A Rare Gift, Genuine Signatures-Autographs, December 1989©
History in the Making, Summer1991©
Love is Contagious, March 8, 1993©
Autographs-African Americans, October 1993©
A Greeting Card-Do You Really Want To Make It,
March 17, 1995©
Letters, Signed, Sealed and Delivered, November7, 1995 ©
The Power of the Mind, 1997©

The Streets Don't Love You Back

"THE STREETS DON'T LOVE YOU BACK"
MOVEMENT
Founder and CEO, Robert D. Boyd Jr.
Co-Founder and President, Lucinda F. Boyd

An afternoon at the Freedom center was emotional
as well as informational.
Don't take your freedom for granted.
"Stand up for something or you'll fall for anything."

The Streets Don't Love You Back

"The Streets Don't Love You Back" Movement Mission Statement

It is our mission to be a force for positive change and inspire others to greatness.

We will trust our dreams and be the prisoner of nothing.

We will strive to continually invent the future out of our imagination rather than be victims of the past.

We will live true to the principles of charity, honesty, integrity, courage, justice, humility, kindness, respect, loyalty to self, trust, knowledge, understanding and non-violence.

We will use our personal defeats and victories unselfishly to help enrich the lives of all who cross our path by caring and affirming their unique worth, by giving what we have to give and teaching them what we know.

We will strive to educate others about the dangers of gang violence and drug activity and that there are many alternatives to the "gang/thug/drug" life.

We will encourage others to rise up and believe that they can be a greater person and believe that they can achieve whatever they want in life.

We will embrace and see each day as not just another day, but one filled with opportunity and excitement as we remember that the pursuit of happiness and excellence will determine the choices we make and the paths we choose to travel.

We choose to make a difference in this world.

There are about 30,000 violent street gangs, motorcycle gangs, and prison gangs with approximately 800,000 members operating in the U.S. today. Many are sophisticated and well organized; all use violence to control neighborhoods and boost their illegal moneymaking activities, which include drug trafficking, robbery, theft, fraud, extortion, prostitution rings, and gun trafficking.
(According to FBI's Violent Gang Taskforce)

*SELLING DRUGS AND THE THUG LIFE IS
THE OLDEST FAILURE IN HISTORY.
THERE HAS NEVER BEEN A SUCCESSFUL
DRUG DEALER/THUG LIFE. A LOT OF
PEOPLE HAVE ALREADY TRIED AND
THEY HAVE ALL FAILED. IN THE END
ALL THEIR STORIES ARE THE SAME. "I
ONCE WAS GETTING OR HAD MILLIONS
AND THEN FIND OUT MY HOME BOY OR
FAMILY MEMBER SET ME UP TO GET
CAUGHT OR KILLED."
IN THE END THEY ALL GET CAUGHT UP.
CHOOSE THE RIGHT PATH IN LIFE MY
PEOPLE AND KNOW THAT THE STREETS
DON'T LOVE YOU BACK AND NEVER
WILL.......LEARN FROM ALL THE OTHERS
WHO HAVE FAILED IN THE STREET LIFE,
IT'S ALL A DEAD END.......DEATH OR LIFE
IN PRISON.........*

Robert D. Boyd Jr.

For more information about:

The Streets Don't Love You Back Movement

The Streets Don't Love You Back Radio Show

The Streets Don't Love You Back TV

The Streets Don't Love You Back Mentoring and Ex-offender Programs

Visit our website at:
www.thestreetsdontloveyouback.com

The Streets Don't Love You Back

The Streets Don't Love You Back

The Streets Don't Love You Back

To Mr & Mrs Tilley

Here is my gift to you both. educating our youths and others to a better life. God bless

Robert L Boyd

10-27-2015